Oxford International Primary

3

Science

Student Book

Deborah Roberts
Terry Hudson

Alan Haigh
Geraldine Shaw

Language consultants:
John McMahon
Liz McMahon

OXFORD

OXFORD
UNIVERSITY PRESS

Great Clarendon Street, Oxford, OX2 6DP, United Kingdom

Oxford University Press is a department of the University of Oxford. It furthers the University's objective of excellence in research, scholarship, and education by publishing worldwide. Oxford is a registered trade mark of Oxford University Press in the UK and in certain other countries.

British Library Cataloguing in Publication Data

Data available

ISBN 978-1-382006569

9 10 8

Paper used in the production of this book is a natural, recyclable product made from wood grown in sustainable forests. The manufacturing process conforms to the environmental regulations of the country of origin.

Printed in China by Golden Cup

Acknowledgements

The publisher and authors would like to thank the following for permission to use photographs and other copyright material:

Cover: Artwork by Blindsalida. **Photos: p12(t):** Wladimir Bulgar/Science Photo Library; **p12(bl):** vavlt/iStockphoto; **p12(br):** Sam Oaksey/Alamy Stock Photo; **p14-15:** dpa picture alliance archive/Alamy Stock Photo; **p15(tl):** Ian Schofield/Shutterstock; **p15(tc):** Vitalii Hulai/Shutterstock; **p15(tr):** Mike Liu/Shutterstock; **p16:** arhip4/Shutterstock; **p17(tl):** AW/Alamy Stock Photo; **p17(tcl):** logoboom/Shutterstock; **p17(tcr):** Beboy/Adobe Stock; **p17(tr):** Ripitya/Shutterstock; **p17(b):** 3445128471/Shutterstock; **p18(t):** Kongsak/Shutterstock; **p18(cl):** Jan Wlodarczyk/Alamy Stock Photo; **p18(cr):** Gordon Bell/Shutterstock; **p20:** JamesChen/Shutterstock; **p22:** Ricardo Reitmeyer/Shutterstock; **p23:** Agefotostock/Alamy Stock Photo; **p24:** Joerg Boethling/Alamy Stock Photo; **p28-29:** Bbbar/Dreamstime.com; **p29(t):** Deejpilot/iStockphoto; **p29(b):** Bas van der Pluijm/Shutterstock; **p30(bl):** Hecos/Alamy Stock Photo; **p30(br):** Zdenek Chaloupka/Shutterstock; **p31(bl):** Josemaria Toscano/Shutterstock; **p31(br):** Bernard Radvaner/Corbis/Getty Images; **p32(t):** Sabena Jane Blackbird/Alamy Stock Photo; **p32(c):** Gyvafoto/Shutterstock; **p32(b):** Tyler Boyes/Shutterstock; **p34:** Arterra Picture Library/Alamy Stock Photo; **p36(bl):** Vitalii Nesterchuk/Shutterstock; **p36(bl):** kavram/Shutterstock; **p36(br):** Karl Kost/Alamy Stock Photo; **p38:** Henfaes/iStockphoto; **p39(t):** Salienko Evgenii/Shutterstock; **p39(b):** pan demin/Shutterstock; **p42(l):** sima/Shutterstock; **p42(r):** Roman Borodaev/Shutterstock; **p44(a):** Dan Breckwoldt/Shutterstock; **p44(b):** Robert Milek/Shutterstock; **p44(c):** BalLi8Tic/Shutterstock; **p44(d):** Kinek00/Shutterstock; **p44(e):** Marjanneke de Jong/Shutterstock; **p44(f):** Kostakirov/Shutterstock; **p44(g):** Free_styler/Alamy Stock Photo; **p44(h):** OKcamera/Shutterstock; **p45:** Bas van der Pluijm/Shutterstock; **p46-47:** Zoonar GmbH/Alamy Stock Photo; **p48:** Design Pics Inc/Alamy Stock Photo; **p50:** Trevor Clifford Photography/Science Photo Library; **p51(tl):** Martin Shields/Alamy Stock Photo; **p51(tr):** Alexandre Dotta/Science Source; **p52:** uniquely india/Getty Images; **p56:** Mark Herreid/Alamy Stock Photo; **p57:** Anest/Shutterstock; **p58:** AnnaKT/Shutterstock; **p60(t):** BetterPhoto/Shutterstock; **p60(b):** Mingkwan Doilom/Shutterstock; **p62:** Zairo/Shutterstock; **p64(tl):** Fremme/Shutterstock; **p64(tr):** Janno Loide/Shutterstock; **p64(b):** inga spence/Alamy Stock Photo; **p67:** Frans Lanting, Mint Images/Science Photo Library; **p68:** Dave Massey/Shutterstock; **p69:** William Mullins/Alamy Stock Photo; **p69:** D Alderman/Alamy Stock Photo; **p69:** Diane Garcia/Shutterstock; **p69:** Merlin D. Tuttle/Science Photo Library; **p69:** Science History Images/Alamy Stock Photo; **p72-73:** Dan Breckwoldt/Shutterstock; **p73:** Simon's passion 4 Travel/Shutterstock; **p74(t):** MariannaSaska/E+/Getty Images; **p74(b):** BruesWu/Moment Open/Getty Images; **p75(t):** Marek Mierzejewski/Shutterstock; **p75(b):** Tom Wang/Shutterstock; **p77:** NASA/Science Photo Library; **p78(tl):** Cultura RM/Alamy Stock Photo; **p78(tr):** Nataly Reinch/Shutterstock; **p78(b):** Haluk Cigsar/Shutterstock; **p79:** Steve Jurvetson/Flickr; **p80(t):** Oleg Znamenskiy/Shutterstock; **p80(b):** Natursports/Shutterstock; **p82:** oksana.perkins/Shutterstock; **p84(r):** Denizo71/Shutterstock; **p84(l):** BrunoRosa/Shutterstock; **p85(l):** My Good Images/Shutterstock; **p85(r):** Oneblink/Dreamstime.com; **p86:** Suphatthra olovedog/Shutterstock; **p87:** European Sports Photo Agency/Alamy Stock Photo; **p88(l):** Pat_Hastings/Shutterstock; **p88(r):** JOEL AREM/Science Photo Library; **p90(t):** Kai Pfaffenbach/Reuters; **p90(c):** Markus Mainka/Shutterstock; **p90(bl):** New Africa/Shutterstock; **p90(br):** Jurik Peter/Shutterstock; **p91(l):** Dorling Kindersley ltd/Alamy Stock Photo; **p91(c):** Stoyanov Alexey/Shutterstock; **p91(r):** Chaiyaphong Kitphaephaisan/123RF; **p93:** AnatolyM/iStockphoto; **p96(a):** Winai Tepsuttinun/Shutterstock; **p96(b):** Ingram Publishing/Alamy Stock Photo; **p96(c):** HABRDA/Shutterstock; **p96(d):** Terekhov Igor/Shutterstock; **p96(e):** Dimedrol68/Shutterstock; **p96(f):** Nils Z/Shutterstock; **p96(g):** Servantes/Shutterstock; **p96(h):** Oxford University Press; **p98(t):** Paul Rapson/Science Photo Library; **p98(b):** Doug Martin/Science Source; **p99(t):** ssuaphotos/Shutterstock; **p99(a):** Pongphan Ruengchai/Alamy Stock Photo; **p99(b):** Kletr/Shutterstock; **p99(c):** Fotocrisis/Shutterstock; **p99(d):** StockPhotosArt - Technology/Alamy Stock Photo; **p102-103:** John M Lund Photography Inc/DigitalVision/Getty Images; **p103:** cynoclub/Shutterstock; **p104(a):** R S Vivek/Dreamstime.com; **p104(b):** Skydive Erick/Shutterstock; **p104(c):** Ivan Taborau/Alamy Stock Photo; **p104(d):** Levent Konuk/Shutterstock; **p104(e):** Ilukee/Alamy Stock Photo; **p105:** Mike Goldwater/Alamy Stock Photo; **p107:** Vectorfair.com/Shutterstock; **p108 & p138(b):** Somogyi Laszlo/Shutterstock; **p110(t):** Philipp1983/Shutterstock; **p110(b):** 3445128471/Shutterstock; **p111:** Art Directors & TRIP/Alamy Stock Photo; **p112(t):** Drazen Zigic/Shutterstock; **p112(b):** Richard Heathcote/Getty Images; **p113:** Phanie/Alamy Stock Photo; **p118:** Omika/Adobe stock; **p118:** Songquan Deng/Shutterstock; **p118(a):** Juniors Bildarchiv GmbH/Alamy Stock Photo; **p118(b):** Zoonar GmbH/Alamy Stock Photo; **p118(c):** massimhokuto/Adobe Stock; **p118(d):** Alex Churilov/Shutterstock; **p121(a):** Tetra Images, LLC/Alamy Stock Photo; **p121(b):** Jovana Dzo/Shutterstock; **p121(c):** Sergey Novikov/Shutterstock; **p121(d):** Marlon Lopez MMG1 Design/Shutterstock; **p124(l):** emmy-images/iStockphoto; **p124(r):** Grzegorz Placzek/Shutterstock; **p124(bl):** Stacy Barnett/Shutterstock; **p124(br):** Valentyn Volkov/Shutterstock; **p125(tl):** srdjan draskovic/Shutterstock; **p125(cl):** Damsea/Shutterstock; **p125(cr):** Amy Johansson/Shutterstock; **p125(tr):** incamerastock/Alamy Stock Photo; **p126:** Photodisc/Getty Images; **p132(tr):** Stephanie Rabemiafara/Art in All of Us/Corbis News/Getty Images; **p132(tl):** Mark Sykes/Science Photo Library; **p133(tr):** Miriam Doerr Martin Frommherz/Shutterstock; **p133(tl):** Zeljko Radojko/Shutterstock; **p136:** Gyvafoto/Shutterstock; **p138(t):** Sabena Jane Blackbird/Alamy Stock Photo; **p138(c):** www.sandatlas.org/Shutterstock.

Artwork by Q2A Media.

Every effort has been made to contact copyright holders of material reproduced in this book. Any omissions will be rectified in subsequent printings if notice is given to the publisher.

Contents

Contents

How to Use this Book

This Student Book for *Oxford International Primary Science* forms part of your science lessons for this year. Your teacher will introduce the ideas through whole-class activities, then you will explore them in more detail using this book, before all coming back together to discuss what you have learned. Find out more at: www.oxfordprimary.com/international-science

Structure of the book

This book is divided into five units plus a *Being a Good Scientist* introduction and a picture Glossary:

Being a Good Scientist
Unit 1 Light and Dark
Unit 2 Looking at Rocks and Soil
Unit 3 Flowering Plants
Unit 4 Introducing Forces and Magnets
Unit 5 Exploring Health, Skeletons and Muscles
Glossary

Each unit covers a different strand of science. You will need a science notebook to write in and to record your investigation results and conclusions.

Being a good scientist

To be a good scientist you need to be curious and ask questions. This section will help you think about how to develop your scientific skills to work like a scientist.

What you will find in each unit

There are three types of lessons:

Wow introduces each unit's scientific ideas and key words. It tells you what you will learn in the unit and lets you discuss what you already know.

Focused lessons cover the scientific knowledge and skills you need to learn this year.

In **What have I learned?** you review your understanding and show your teacher what you have learned about the unit.

What you will find in the lessons

Although each lesson is unique, they have common features:

The words on the Wow pages are included in the picture glossary at the back of the book. You can add your own notes for each word.

Key words
water
wilt

Gives you the key words for the lesson.

In this lesson you will explore some of the uses and strength of magnets. Tells you what you will learn in the lesson.

Questions to help you talk to each other and share ideas about the science you are learning and the investigations you do.

Practical and research activities to investigate and report on science topics. Sometimes your teacher will ask you to use different equipment, which is available in school. They may also ask you to carry out a test in a different way, to make sure you are safe.

Stretch zone Challenges you to take your learning further.

Key idea Summarises what you have learned.

Additional features

Think back Reminds you what has been covered before.

Science fact Interesting and amazing science facts.

Highlights the skills needed to be a good scientist.

Important notes about how to stay safe.

Teacher's Guide

There is a Teacher's Guide to help your teacher to work out the resources needed and to offer alternative activities and approaches.

Workbook

At the bottom of each page in this book is a link to a Workbook, where you can record your work and get extra practice to do in your lesson or at home.

Being a Good Scientist

Science is the study of the world around us. To be a good scientist you need to be curious and ask questions. This section will help you think about how to develop your scientific skills to work like a scientist.

Scientists look carefully at the world to explain why things happen and to guess if things may happen. Science is used to develop new technologies. It also helps us know more about health and diseases. This means we can develop medicines and machines to keep people healthy.

You will have to make decisions about the type of scientific investigations you should be doing and which observations you should be carrying out. You will need to bring all of your skills together to plan and carry out fair tests and to record and present your findings.

The diagram shows the steps you can take to plan and carry out investigations like a scientist. This builds on the steps you have already learned about how to work scientifically.

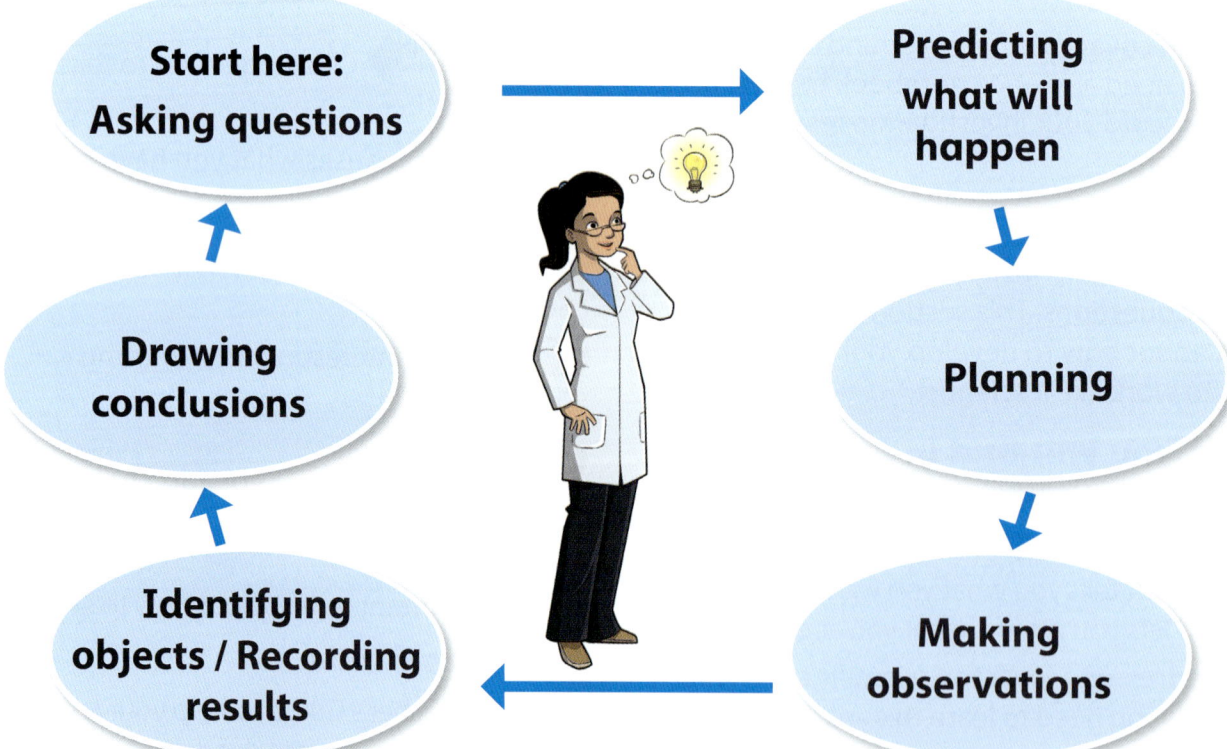

Learning to be a scientist allows you to develop scientific skills such as observing (looking), measuring and recording. It helps you to notice patterns in the things you observe and to sort things into groups. It also helps you to test your own ideas about how the world works.

Asking questions

Scientists ask questions about the world around them. This is called scientific enquiry.

A good way to start is to think of questions that start with words such as 'which', 'what', 'why', 'how', 'do' and 'does'. Your questions should lead you towards planning an investigation or carrying out research to find out more about a subject.

How are these plants different?

Why are they different?

Think of your own questions to ask about the plants. Think about different factors such as light or water.

The questions you ask will give you a good start to your investigation.

Questions can also come out of the results of an investigation. For example, when investigating plants you might observe that some grew well with very little light. What questions would these results make you think about?

That is why the investigation process is shown in a circle. Each investigation can lead to new questions to investigate.

Predicting what will happen

Next, scientists try to work out what will happen. Scientists call this a prediction.

They need to talk about their ideas and think about what they already know about a topic. You might have already learned something about the question you are trying to answer. Scientists usually know something before they make predictions.

Use what you know about shadows to help you think about this question.

What would you observe if you looked at a shadow in the morning, at midday, and in the afternoon?

Do you think the shadow would change? What did you think about to help you decide?

As a scientist, you draw on your previous experiences. Think about when you have seen shadows. You could also think about why people move during a day to keep out of the Sun. This makes your prediction much better than a guess. It is based on scientific knowledge and evidence.

Scientists often use **models** to represent objects or the way things work. Models help scientists to think about new ideas, things that cannot be seen or happened a long time ago. For example, you can model how different types of fossils were formed. Scientists use models to make predictions and to explain observations.

Planning

Scientists plan what they are going to do. They always discuss their plans before they start. This helps them to check that the plan will work.

You will be encouraged to set up what are called **comparative tests**. This is when you design an investigation to compare different things. For example, you might want to compare the strengths of different magnets.

How are the students comparing the magnets?

Why are they not adding paperclips to one magnet and pins to the other?

It is important that an investigation is a **fair test**. Scientists make their investigations fair by following some simple rules.

- They think about what they will keep the same.

- They think about what they will change.

For example, when investigating the strength of magnets, you should use the same material to test each one. If you use paperclips for one magnet, you have to use paperclips for the other. You should add them in the same way – it would not be a fair test if you added them end-to-end on one magnet and as a cluster on the other. This makes sure that the only change is the strength of the magnet.

Scientists think about the **equipment** they need. They make a list and make sure everything is available. For example, if you are going to test the strength of forces you might make a list like this:

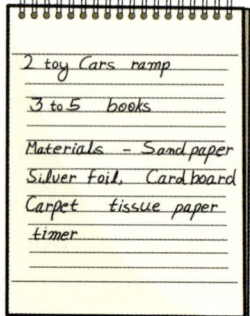

2 toy cars ramp

3 to 5 books

Materials – Sand paper
Silver foil, Cardboard
Carpet tissue paper
timer

Science fact

Scientists do not always plan their own investigations. Sometimes they follow other scientists' plans. This is why it is very important to make plans easy to follow.

Sometimes it is not possible to plan an investigation to answer your questions. For example, if you want to know about rocks deep inside the Earth, you will not be able to travel there to observe them. You will have to use other sources of information such as the internet, books and magazines. These are called **secondary sources of information**.

When have you used secondary sources to find out more about science?

What were they? How did you use them?

Making observations

Scientists use their observation skills during investigations.

> What are the different senses you can use when observing investigations? Why do you have to be careful when using these senses?

Scientists do not just observe investigations when they have a bit of time. They plan carefully to make observations at the right times. They use computers, data loggers and other devices, such as smartphones and electronic scales, to help them to take accurate measurements.

They are very careful to use standard units to record their results. Standard units allow people from all over the world to understand and compare the results. For example, when measuring plant heights, they would use units of millimetres or centimetres or metres. They would not use grams or degrees.

> Which standard units would you use to measure:
>
> a) temperature,
>
> b) the distance between villages,
>
> c) the amount of flour needed in a recipe?

You may need to use equipment to help with your observations. Some of the pieces of equipment you will use this year are shown below.

Good scientists take a measurement more than once. This is to make sure they have not made any mistakes. They then find out the average for their readings. The example below shows the results of an investigation.

Animal	Number of animals found under a stone			
	Count 1	Count 2	Count 3	Average
woodlouse	2	8	5	
ant	3	1	2	
worm	1	1	1	

> What should the average results be for each animal? Which animal was the most common under the stone? Why was it useful to not just take the first readings?

To identify objects you may use a key. This is a diagram with simple questions.

As you answer the questions it moves you closer to the object you are trying to identify.

Keys are used a lot in science to help identify living things. Look at this key.

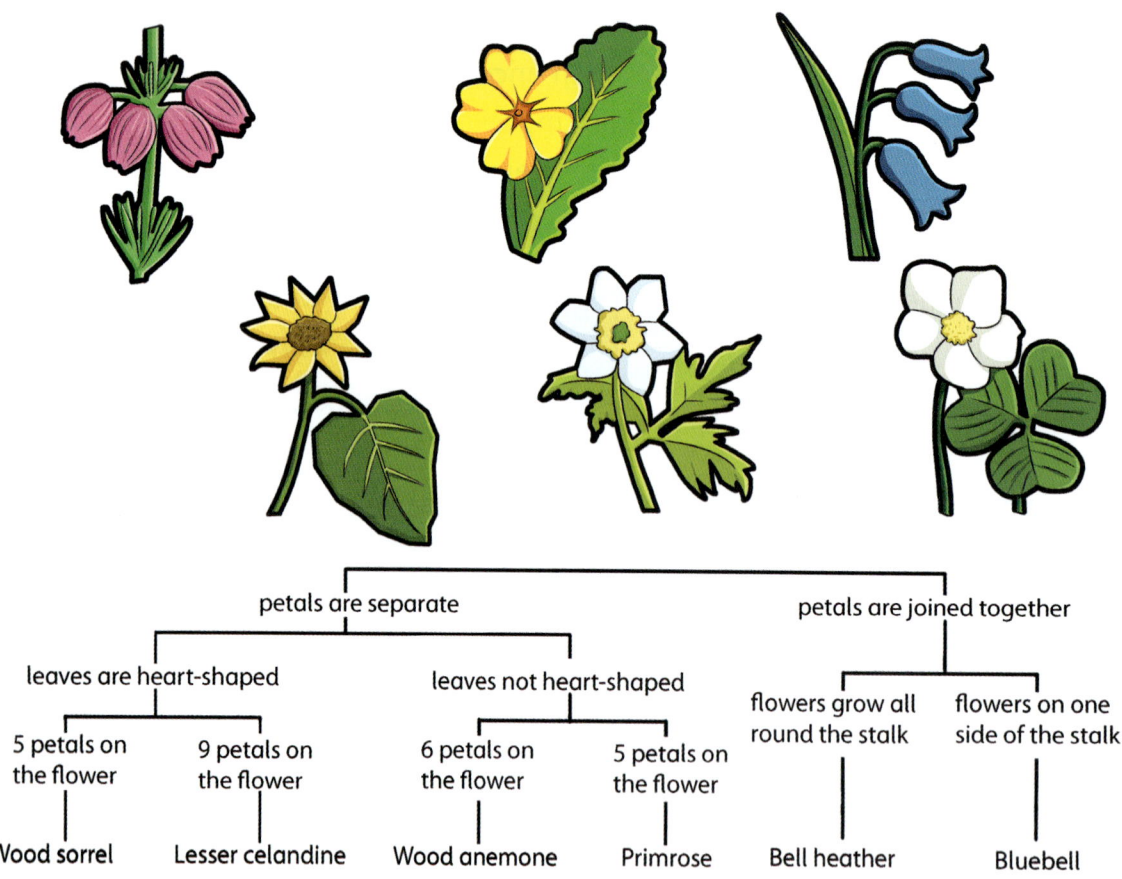

Identify the flowers using the key.

Why are keys so useful?

Recording results

Scientists write down or record what they have found from their observations and measurements. This helps them to see patterns or to sort things into groups.

You will need to use your results to draw conclusions. If you do not record your results carefully, you may not be able to make the most sensible conclusions. There are lots of different ways to record results.

Tables

One way to record results is to complete a table.

You could use a table like this one to record what happens to the size of a shadow as the object casting the shadow is moved towards the screen and away from the light source.

Distance between object and screen (centimetres)	Size of shadow (centimetres)
0	20
10	25
20	35
30	40
40	50
50	55

Look at the table. Answer these questions with your partner.

What is the biggest size the shadow becomes?

What is the smallest size of the shadow?

Describe any patterns you can see in the results.

Charts

Results from tables can be shown as charts or graphs.

This chart shows the results of the shadow investigation.

The size of the shadow is plotted from bottom to top on this chart.

The distance between the object and the screen is plotted along the bottom.

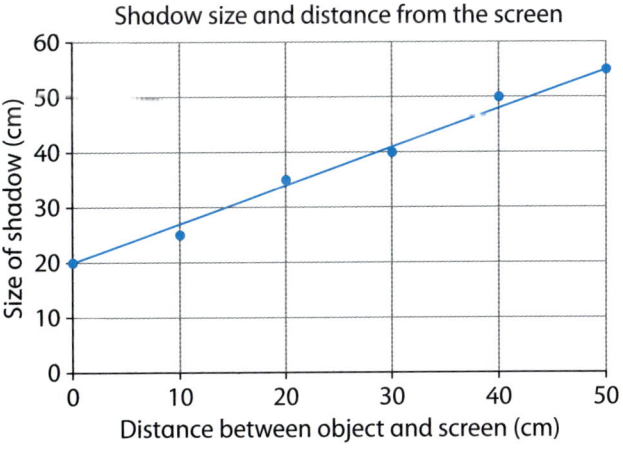

Shadow size and distance from the screen

Do you think this chart is easier or harder to read from than the table of results?

Using charts can sometimes make it easier to see patterns in the results.

Drawings, photographs and videos

You have worked with scientific drawings before. Remember they are not like the pictures you paint. Scientific drawings are much simpler.

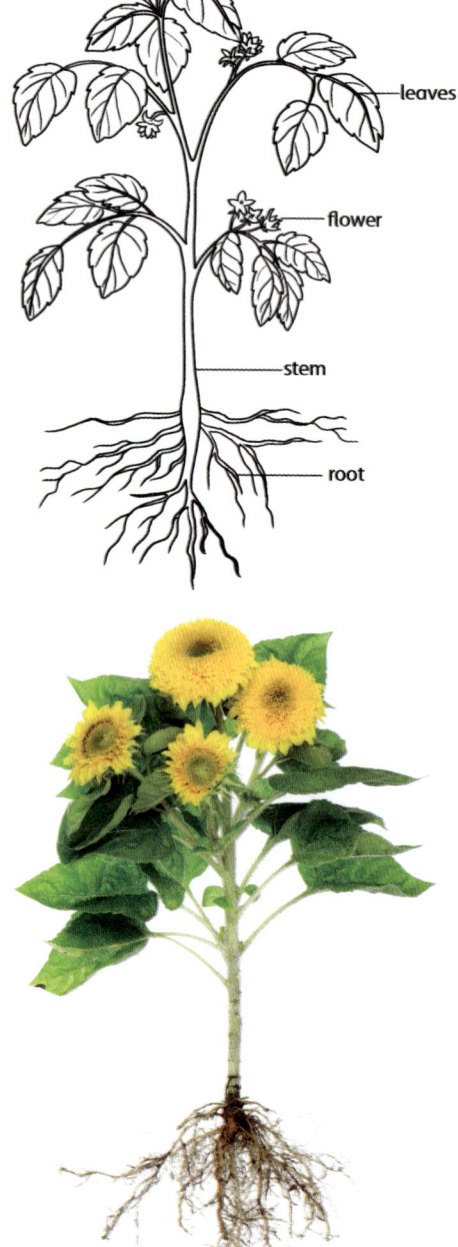

Scientists also use modern technology to take photographs and video clips of their investigations and results.

Photographs show a lot of detail

This is a very accurate way to record results. This level of detail would not be possible without using a camera.

Filming also allows scientists to see things that may be impossible to see in person, such as the behaviour of these eagles in their nest.

Tiny cameras can be placed where we can't observe with our eyes

How could you use a camera or a video recorder to observe what happens as a car rolls down a ramp?

When scientists are observing and measuring living things, they take great care of the environment. They try not to damage the places where animals live. They do not pick too many plants. They return small animals back to where they were. They do this as gently as they can to make sure the animals are unharmed.

Drawing conclusions

The last stage of an investigation is when scientists look at their results carefully. It is at this stage that they make sense of their results. They work out if the results have helped them to answer their investigation question.

The questions they might ask are:

Can I *see* any patterns?

Are any results unusual?

Was my prediction correct?

Scientists also link their conclusions to bigger scientific ideas. For example, if they are thinking about the animals they have found in a habitat, they will link this to the foods the animals eat and what eats them. They will also think about other factors, such as how much water there is and how warm or cold it is.

After completing an investigation, a good scientist will study their results and think about what went well and what could be improved. This is called evaluation and is an important part of the investigation process. Here are some reminder notes a scientist might use.

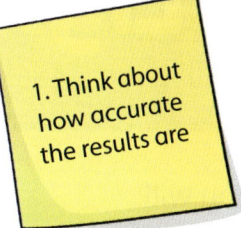

1. Think about how accurate the results are

They will try to work out ways to improve their investigation.

2. Report the findings to others

They do this by talking to others, writing a report or making a display. This might be a poster or a computer presentation. They may include models.

Scientists are very careful to use the correct scientific language. This makes their ideas much clearer. They also plan their reports and presentations to match their audience. For example, if they are talking to people who are not scientists, they will not include as much detail as they would in a scientific paper.

3. Think about any new questions that the investigation has raised

For example, if they studied different animals in a habitat, they would think about whether that could be linked to the different plants that also live there.

It is useful to fill out an investigation planning form. This sets out all the stages of your investigation. It helps you to remember everything you need to think about. Your teacher can give you one of these.

1 Light and Dark

In this unit you will:

- find out about different light sources
- discover that darkness is when there is no light
- notice that light is reflected from some surfaces
- understand how people protect their eyes from the Sun
- find out how shadows are made
- explore and find patterns in shadows.

dark light pattern protect reflect shadow Sun torch

Work with a partner and talk about the photograph.

The sailors are looking for people in the water.

Why do you think they are using a search light?

Look at the photographs of the animal eyes.

Are they all the same size and colour?

Look at your partner's eyes. Do they look like the eyes in the photographs?

Science fact

Light travels at 300 million metres every second. That is very fast!

Stretch zone

Some fish that live deep in the ocean do not have eyes.

Tell your partner why you think this is.

■ For more activities, go to Workbook 3 pages 14–15.

Where does light come from?

In this lesson you will find out about different light sources, including the Sun.

Key words

human-made

light

natural

protect

source

Sun

Think back

Have you ever seen lightning during a thunderstorm?

Lightning is a source of light

A source of light is something that makes its own light.

We need light so we can see things.

 Thinking about light sources

The man in the picture is trying to read his newspaper using lightning as a light source.

1 Look at the words in the box below. Point to each word and read it aloud.

2 Which of these things would be a better source of light for the man to use?

You may choose more than one.

> candle   flower   light bulb   mirror   shiny spoon   torch

3 Name an important source of light that is not in the word box above.

Talk to your partner about why this might not be a good idea.

16

■ For more activities, go to Workbook 3 page 16.

| Sun | street light | volcano | candle |

Some sources of light are natural like the Sun, stars and volcanoes.

Some things made by people also give out light. These are human-made objects like torches, lamps, street lights and candles.

 Investigating sources of light

Work with a partner. Look at the photographs above.

1 Talk about the source of light in each one. Which ones would be good for the man to use to read his paper?

2 Make a list of all the sources of light you may find in a room.

Stretch zone

Sort the list of light sources into natural light sources and human-made light sources.

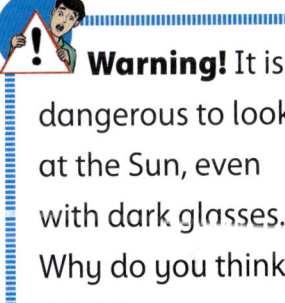 **Warning!** It is dangerous to look at the Sun, even with dark glasses. Why do you think this is?

How do sunglasses protect people's eyes from sunlight?

Key ideas

- Some objects give out light.
- Sources of light can be natural or human-made.

1 Light and Dark

17

■ For more activities, go to Workbook 3 page 17.

Is a mirror a source of light?

In this lesson you will explore objects that reflect light.

It is night-time in the first photograph, but the people can see each other.

Key words
light
reflect

How can these people see each other?

Where is the light coming from?

There are some shiny things that we think are sources of light, but they are not.

They 'bounce' or reflect the light from another source to our eyes. This is called reflection.

Look at these buildings. The shiny surfaces are reflecting the light.

Where have you seen or used a mirror?

Talk to your partner about what a mirror looks like.

Have you ever touched a mirror?

What did it feel like?

18

■ For more activities, go to Workbook 3 page 18.

Does a mirror give out light?

In this investigation you will explore whether a mirror is a source of light.

1   With a partner, take it in turns to hold a mirror in front of your face to look at your reflection.

2   Your teacher will change the amount of light in the room.

    Predict what you will see.

Be a scientist

Scientists predict (guess) what will happen using their knowledge and experience.

▶ page 7

What happens to your reflection when there is no light in the room?

There are many things that appear bright but they are just reflections of light from somewhere else.

The Moon and shiny objects behave like this.

Reflection or a light source?

1   Look at the pictures. Read the words aloud.

    Talk to your partner.

2   Which of these do you think are sources of light?

3   Which of these do you think just reflect light?

| planet | Sun | mirror | spoon | candle |

Key idea

Shiny surfaces, like mirrors, are not sources of light.

They reflect light from another source.

Stretch zone

Why do you think people might place a mirror opposite a window in a room? Draw a picture to explain your thoughts.

■ For more activities, go to Workbook 3 page 19.

What is darkness?

In this lesson you will discover that darkness is when there is no light.

Key words
dark/light

Think back

Think back to your learning about human-made light. Tell your partner about three human-made sources of light that might help you to see well.

At night there is not a lot of natural light. It is dark.

Talk to your partner about seeing in the dark.

What can you see in a dark room?

■ For more activities, go to Workbook 3 page 20.

When the Sun goes down, or you switch off a light, there is no longer a source of light.

We call this darkness.

The light can no longer send information to our eyes so we find it difficult to see.

How could you test this?

Investigating darkness

Your teacher will make a room that can be used as a dark room.

Sit down in the place where you are asked to.

Warning!

Do not get up or move around during the investigation. Discuss why this is important.

1 Look around the room when the lights are on. Try to remember where some objects are.

2 Your teacher will remove all the sources of light so that the room is in darkness. Think about how it feels in the dark.

3 When there is a source of light, talk about these questions with your group:
- Could you see anything?
- Could you see any light?
- Where did the light come from?
- Could you see any of the objects you tried to remember?
- Could you hear any sounds?

Stretch zone

Write a sentence to explain how you can stop the light you can see getting into the dark room.

Key idea

When there is no light, we say it is dark.

■ For more activities, go to Workbook 3 page 21.

We need light to see things

In this lesson you will explore the idea that we need light to see.

Key words
dark/light
dim

Think back

What is the difference between light and dark?

How can you still see things at night?

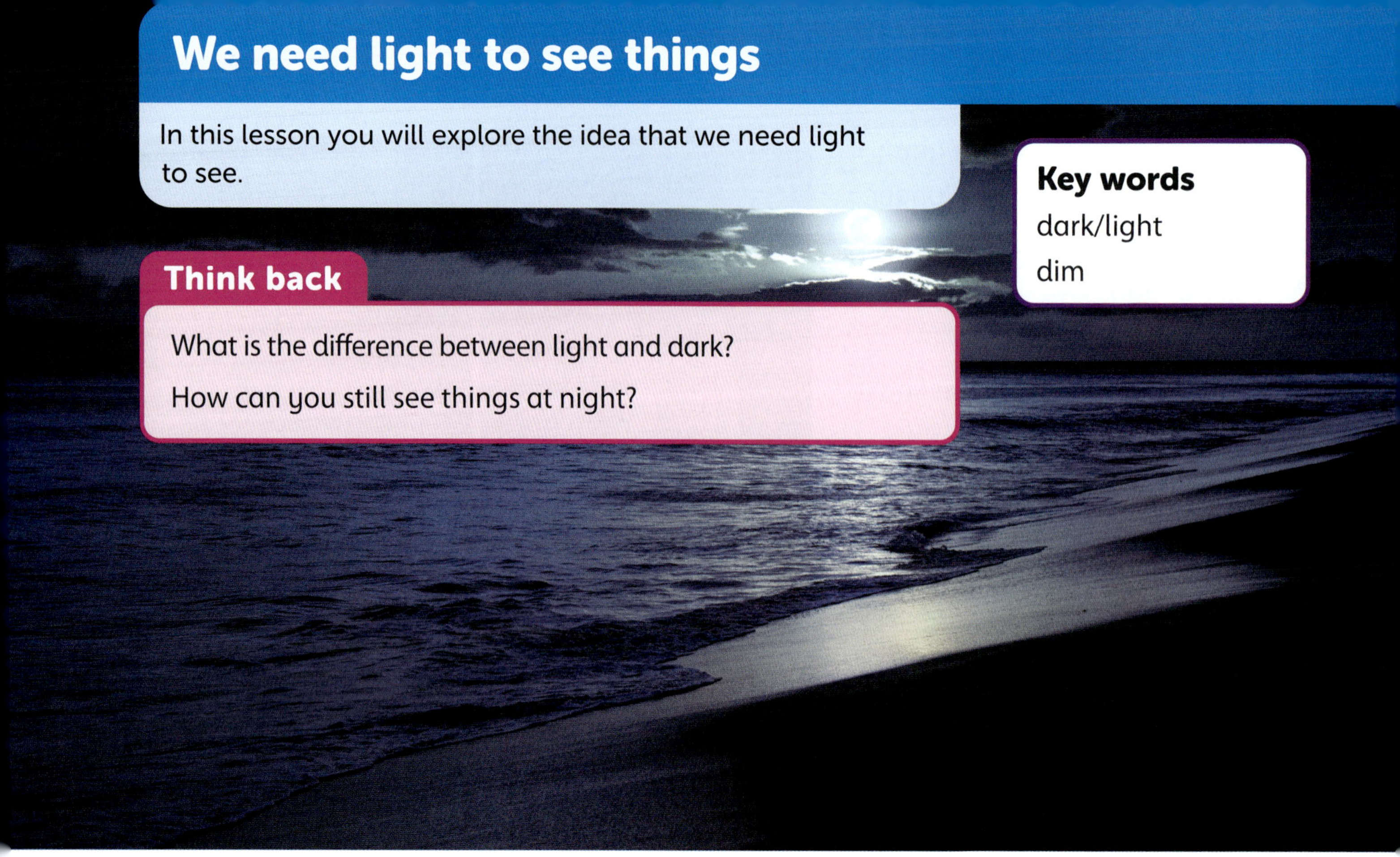

Do we need light to move around safely?

1 Tie a blindfold over your eyes and try to move around the room.

2 Ask your partner to help you so you don't bump into things.

3 Now let your partner have a go and you help them move around safely.

Talk to your partner about how it felt to move around when you couldn't see. Was it easy or difficult?

Warning! Be careful when you are blindfolded. Walk slowly with your arms in front of you.

Be a scientist

Good scientists plan their investigations carefully to find out if the information they are given is true.

▶ page 8

In dim light, the holes (called pupils) at the front of our eyes get bigger. This lets more light in and helps us to see better when it starts to get dark.

How could you prove this?

22

 For more activities, go to Workbook 3 page 22.

Is all light the same?

1 Try to read this page in the dark.

2 Then use candlelight.

3 Now try it with a torch.

What did you find? When was it easier to read the page?

 Warning! Don't touch the lit candle. What could happen if you did this?

Some animals get a picture of what is around them by hearing, so they don't need light.

They make a clicking sound. The sound bounces back to them from buildings and other objects.

Bats 'see' like this.

 Can you 'see' by making a clicking sound?

Work with a partner for this investigation.

1 Practise making a clicking sound with your tongue. If you cannot do this, use the on and off button on a pen.

2 Take it in turns to be blindfolded. While blindfolded, make your clicking sound as your partner slowly guides you around the room.

3 Tell your partner when you think you are in front of an object or an open space.

4 After your investigation talk about what it was like to move around using clicking sounds.

5 How did you know when you were in front of an object or an open space?

6 Would you like to move around in this way?

Imagine you had no natural light. What would you miss seeing?

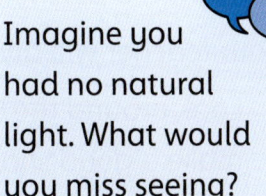

Key idea

At night, when there is no sunlight and it is dark, we use other sources of light to see.

Some blind people use this clicking technique to move about every day.

■ For more activities, go to Workbook 3 page 23.

1 Light and Dark

Investigating shadows

In this lesson you will learn how shadows are made and explore how they change size.

Key words

opaque

pattern

shadow

torch

Think back

You can see shadows in the day and at night.

Where is the light coming from? What is making the shade?

Parts of the street are in the light. Other parts are in the shade.

An object that does not let light through is called opaque.

When light from any source is blocked by an object it forms a dark patch. This is called a shadow.

What makes a good shadow?

Work with a partner to make shadows.

Your teacher will give you a torch to use as a source of light.

1 Look around the room and find objects that you think will make a good shadow.

2 Shine the torch on each object. Does it make a good shadow?

3 Draw around the best shadow you make on a clean piece of paper.

Be a scientist

A good scientist would try each object more than once and record their results before deciding which is the best shadow.

▶ page 9

Stretch zone

Can you describe, to your partner, the type of objects that make the best shadows?

■ For more activities, go to Workbook 3 page 24.

Sometimes we make shadows for fun.

Using your hand to make a shadow

1 Stand in front of a wall or a flat surface.

2 Hold your hand in front of a lit torch.

3 Try making different shapes with your fingers.

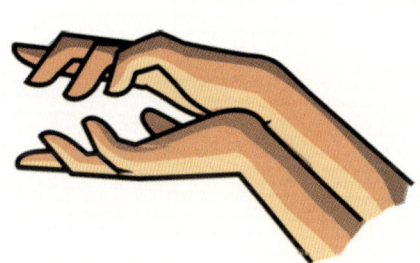  

4 If you hold the torch very close to your hand what happens to the shadow?

What happens if you hold the torch further away?

5 Record your findings. Is there a pattern in your results?

 Stretch zone

Is a shadow always the same shape as the object that makes it? Tell your teacher your thoughts.

Check how much you know.
Try the questions on pages 26–27.

Key ideas

- When light is blocked by an object it makes a shadow.
- Shadows can change size and shape.

■ For more activities, go to Workbook 3 page 25.

What have I learned about light and dark?

1 **a** Colour in the words that are sources of light.

spoon   candle   mirror

Sun   torch   door

b Tick a source of light made by people.

2 Underline one of these sentences to best describe darkness.

Darkness is when there is a little light.

Darkness is when there is bright light.

Darkness is when there is no light.

3 What would be the best source of light for reading a book? Tick one.

candle light ☐

sunlight ☐

moonlight ☐

4 Decide whether each statement is true or false. Circle your answers.

Shadows are only made by the Sun.   true   false

Shadows are formed when an object blocks light.   true   false

Shadows never change size.   true   false

■ For more activities, go to Workbook 3 page 26.

5 Circle the object that would make the darkest shadow.

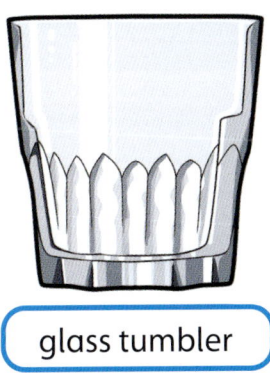

glass tumbler

plastic tumbler

metal tumbler

6 Which of these positions show where you should hold a torch to make the longest shadow? Tick your answer.

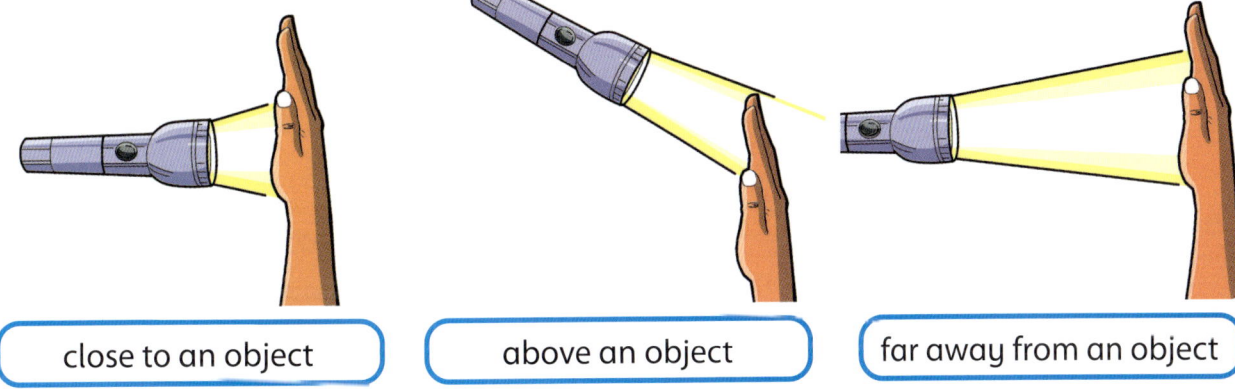

close to an object

above an object

far away from an object

7 Describe one way we can protect our eyes from the Sun.

_____

8 **a** Circle the examples of objects that reflect light.

b A student says: 'The Moon is a source of light at night-time.' Do you agree? Explain your answer.

_____

_____

■ For more activities, go to Workbook 3 page 27.

2 Looking at Rocks and Soil

In this unit you will:

- name some types of rock
- compare and group rocks by what they look like and other properties
- learn how fossils are formed
- investigate different types of soil.

Science fact

The oldest rocks on Earth are nearly four billion years old.

crystal   fossil   grain
group   property
rock   sand
soil   stone

Look at the photograph of the building.

With a partner, compare it to the rock tower in the main photograph.

What are both made from?

Imagine you could use the material of the rock tower for buildings. Why would it be useful? Why might it cause problems?

What do you think this is?

How old do you think it is? Is it hundreds, thousands, hundreds of thousands, millions or billions of years old?

29

■ For more activities, go to Workbook 3 pages 28–29.

What are rocks?

In this lesson you will find out about rocks and where they are found.

The Earth is made up of layers. As you move towards the inner core, it gets hotter and hotter.

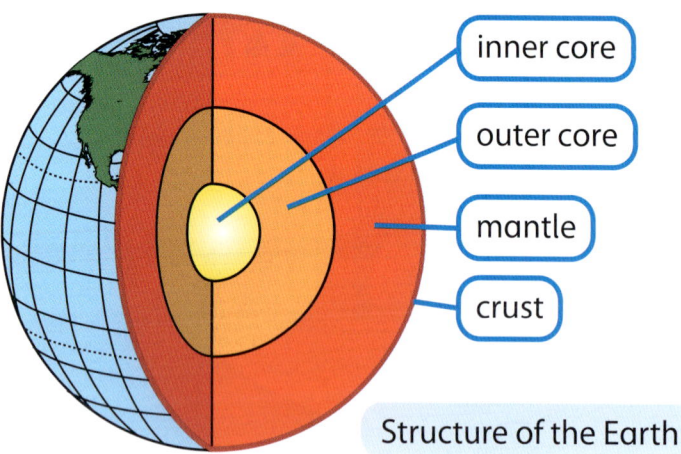

- inner core
- outer core
- mantle
- crust

Structure of the Earth

Key words
pebble
rock
sand
stone

All of the rocks we use are only from the upper layer. This is the thin crust.

Under the oceans the crust is even thinner. Hot, molten rock can rise up from the mantle. It cools to form new rock.

Stretch zone

Use modelling clay to make a model of the Earth's structure. Find out how thick the layers are and make sure you show this in your model.

Look at the photographs. Why is rock such a good material for this use? What do the photographs tell you about how hardwearing rock is?

Rocks are found everywhere and we can see them all around us.

Small stones that you find on the ground are broken down pieces of rock. Smooth, rounded stones are called pebbles.

Sand is also made from rock. It is tiny grains of rock that have been broken down by the weather.

■ For more activities, go to Workbook 3 page 30.

Survey of rocks in your area

Your teacher will take you around the school and the school grounds.

1 Find different ways that rocks are used.

2 Use a checklist like this to record each place you found rocks being used:

for walls ☐

for roofs ☐

for steps ☐

for decoration ☐

for containers or pots ☐

3 Add any other uses to your checklist if you find them.

Warning! Listen carefully to the instructions from your teacher so that you stay safe.

Be a scientist

Scientists make careful observations and record their findings clearly when carrying out surveys.

▶ page 9

Rocks are also found under the ground and at the bottom of the sea.

Stretch zone

What is under the school? If you dug down deep enough, what might you find? Tell your partner.

Key idea

Rocks have many uses and are found everywhere.

■ For more activities, go to Workbook 3 page 31.

Types of rock

In this lesson you will find out about different types of rock.

Think back

Think back to what you learned about properties of materials.

- Name two natural materials used in buildings.
- Name two human-made materials used in buildings.

Key words

crystal

grain

group

igneous

metamorphic

rock cycle

sedimentary

Rocks form in different ways. Different types of rock have different properties.

Sedimentary rock

Sedimentary rock forms when small grains of rock are washed into the sea and settle in layers. Examples are sandstone and mudstone. Some sedimentary rock forms when living things die. Shells and bones can settle to the bottom of the sea. This makes limestone. Sedimentary rocks have tiny spaces between the grains. This allows water to move through them.

sandstone

Igneous rock

Some rocks form when hot, liquid rocks cool down. This type of rock is called igneous rock. Examples are granite and basalt. These rocks do not have separate grains. They are made up of crystals, are usually hard, and do not let water through.

granite

Metamorphic rock

Igneous and sedimentary rock can be heated and squashed deep inside the Earth over many years. This changes them into a new type of rock called metamorphic rock. Examples are marble and slate. They are usually hard and do not allow water through.

slate

What is one difference between granite and limestone?

■ For more activities, go to Workbook 3 page 32.

The formation and breaking down of rocks is a cycle.

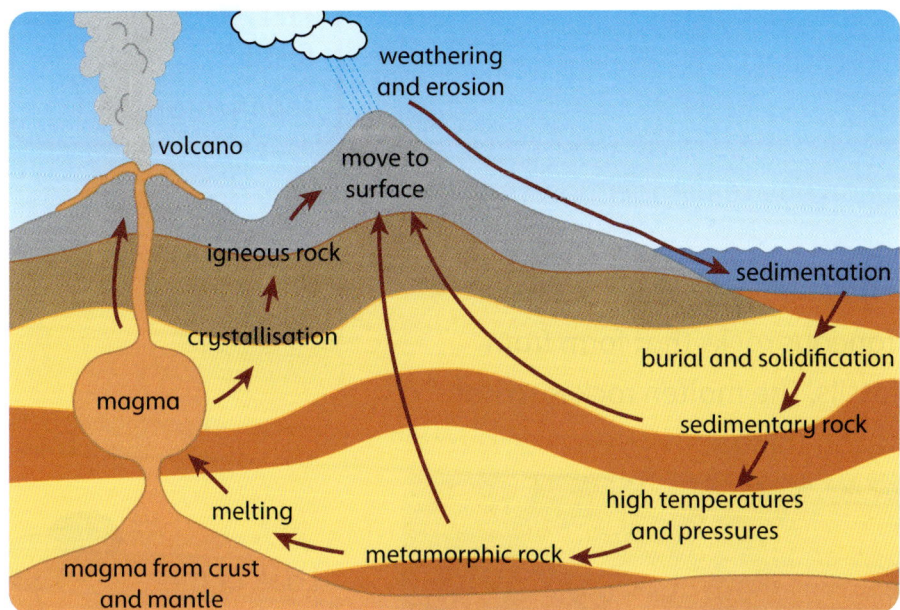

The rock cycle

Rain, snow, wind and ice break down rocks. This is called weathering.

The weakened rock can be worn away. This is called erosion.

Making the rock cycle

1 Work in a group to make your own large diagram or model of the rock cycle for a class display.

2 On your diagram or model, write down where and how igneous, metamorphic and sedimentary rocks are formed.

Grouping rock samples

You are going to compare and group some rock samples.

You will need a hand lens or magnifying glass.

1 Look at the rock samples. Record all your findings in a table.

2 Observe the colour and hardness of each rock.

3 Are the rocks made of grains or crystals? What size are the grains or crystals?

4 Record if you can see fossils or layers.

5 Use a rock identification book or key to help you to name your rocks.

6 Make a rock display. Draw the rocks or take photographs. Add labels to show the type of rock and how it might have formed.

Key ideas

- Different types of rocks form in different ways.
- Rocks can be grouped according to their properties.

■ For more activities, go to Workbook 3 page 33.

How fossils form

In this lesson you will find out that fossils form when things that have lived become trapped within rock.

Think back

Rocks form in different ways. Can you remember how the three types of rock form?

Molten rock is hot, liquid rock. Igneous rocks that form from molten rock cannot have any fossils. The molten rock is so hot that it destroys the remains of living things.

Look at the fossils in this rock. How do you think they got there?

Sedimentary rocks are made when small pieces of sediment (sand or mud) settle to the bottom of the sea. This rock can have fossils. This happens when animals or plants die and are gently covered up by layers. The process takes millions of years.

The dinosaur settles on the bottom of the ocean	Sediments build up on top of it	An impression of the dinosaur is made in the rock

How fossils form

Body fossils show the hard parts of what was once the living thing, such as shells, teeth and bones. Trace fossils are signs that a living thing was once present. Trace fossils include leaf impressions, footprints or even tail marks.

Fossils help scientists to research plants and animals that lived a long time ago.

Science fact

Scientists who study life that existed many years ago are called palaeontologists.

■ For more activities, go to Workbook 3 page 34.

Observing fossils

Your teacher will give you some samples of sedimentary rock and a hand lens.

1 With your partner, look closely at the sample.

2 Draw a diagram of any fossils you observe.

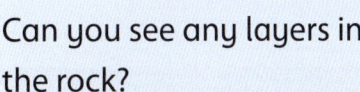

Can you see any layers in the rock?

Discuss with your partner how living things could become trapped.

Making model fossils

Part 1

1 Take a piece of dough.

2 Press objects into it and cover them with another layer of dough. Use model animals or leaves if you can find them.

3 Leave the objects inside the dough and let it dry.

4 Pass your dough to another person. Let them dig for fossils.

Part 2

1 Use another piece of dough.

2 This time press your objects into the surface only to make an impression.

3 Remove the objects. You have made a mould.

4 Your teacher will pour a small amount of wax or chocolate into your mould.

How does your investigation show two different ways that fossils can be made?

Stretch zone

Research some fossils that have been found in your area. Think about information you could get from local museums. Make a poster of your findings.

Key ideas

- Fossils occur when living things become trapped in rock.
- Fossils form over millions of years.

■ For more activities, go to Workbook 3 page 35.

Rocks as building materials

In this lesson you will explore how rock can be used as a building material.

Key words
brick
concrete
glass
human-made
metal
natural
plastic

The photograph shows an ancient city. What is it made from?

Rocks have been used for buildings for thousands of years. The rock is often cut into smooth blocks. Rock has also been used for making roads and bridges, and for carrying water from one place to another.

These rocks have been helping to carry water for thousands of years

Modern stone buildings are strong and beautiful

Look at the photographs above.

Discuss the different ways that rocks are being used.

Discuss the reasons why rock is such a useful material.

■ For more activities, go to Workbook 3 page 36.

Rock is a natural building material. Other natural building materials are wood, clay, straw and bamboo.

Be a scientist

Scientists use their investigation skills to make and test new materials to be used in construction.

▶ page 6

Making bricks

Clay can be used to make building bricks.

1 Squash some clay in your hands until it feels nice and soft.

2 Press the clay with your hands until it is the shape of a brick.

3 Leave the clay to dry. It will make a hard brick.

4 Test your brick to see how hard it is.

Does your brick break easily?

Can you scrape pieces from it?

How does it compare to rocks near your school?

Why might bricks be more useful than natural rock?

Not all building materials are natural. Some are made by people. These are human-made materials like glass, bricks, plastic, concrete and metals.

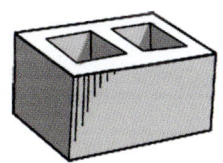

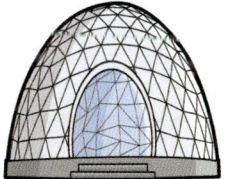

concrete blocks   clay bricks   plastic dome   metal bars   glass bricks

Look at the pictures. Which are used in your school?

Science fact

It is estimated that 50 billion tonnes of sand and gravel are taken from the Earth every year for building!

Key idea

The use of rock as a building material has changed over time.

■ For more activities, go to Workbook 3 page 37.

More about uses of rocks

In this lesson you will explore further how rocks can be used in different ways.

Key words
hard/soft
property

Think back

Think about the rocks you have studied so far. Which type of rock contains sand grains? Which rock contains sea shells? Which rocks are made from crystals?

Some of the rocks you tested were very hard. These would be good for building houses and roads.

Other rocks look nice. These can be used for the front of buildings or for tiled floors.

Other rocks are too soft to be used for building.

Look at the photograph. The man is splitting a type of rock called slate.

Why do you think this rock is good for covering roofs to keep rain out?

Which rocks would be best for making steps?

Imagine a new hospital is being built near to your school.

Your science team have been asked to test rocks to find the best one for building the hospital steps.

1 Discuss the properties that you want the rock to have.

2 Plan a way to test the different possible rocks.

3 Carry out your tests.

4 Record your findings. You may want to design a results table.

5 Write an e-mail to the people building the hospital. Describe how you tested the rocks.

Recommend one of the rocks. Give your reasons.

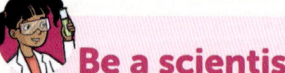

Be a scientist
Scientists plan investigations to test their ideas. They might need to carry out many tests to make sure their findings are right.

▶ page 8

■ For more activities, go to Workbook 3 page 38.

Rocks used for buildings and roads are dug out of the ground in quarries. Sand and gravel can be taken from riverbeds. Some rocks are taken out of deep holes called mines.

As well as being used for building, rocks are also a source of other important materials. Oil, natural gas and metals, such as iron and aluminium, are found in rocks. To find these materials, people have to drill or dig into rock in the Earth's crust.

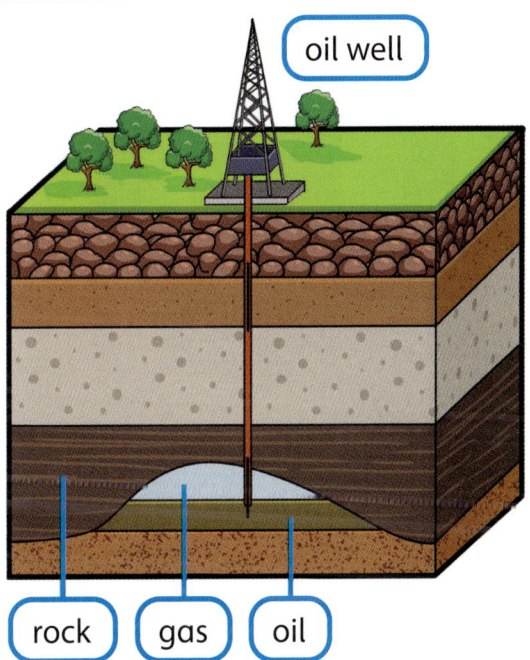

oil well

rock   gas   oil

People are drilling into this rock to find oil

What would your life be like if oil, gas and metals were not found in rocks?

Stretch zone

Find out how iron is taken out of rock in the Earth's crust. Write a short report to share with the class.

Key ideas

- Different rocks are used for different things depending on their properties.
- Rock is the source of some important materials.

■ For more activities, go to Workbook 3 page 39.

What is soil?

In this lesson you will find out that soil forms from broken down rocks.

Key words
clay
humus
sand
soil

Think back

What do plants need to help them to grow?

Look at the picture. What are the people doing?

With a partner, write down the names of three plants that you have each eaten this week.

Plants need something to grow in. This is a special mixture called soil. Soil provides plants with food, water and support.

Look at the people in the picture again.
How are they using the soil?

Science fact

Only 7.5% of the Earth's surface is soil. That is why it is so important to protect soil and not remove or damage it.

■ For more activities, go to Workbook 3 page 40.

Soil has small pieces of rock in it. These can be as small as sand grains or as large as pebbles.

Soil has lots of different things in it to help plants grow. The dead plants and animals in soil are called humus.

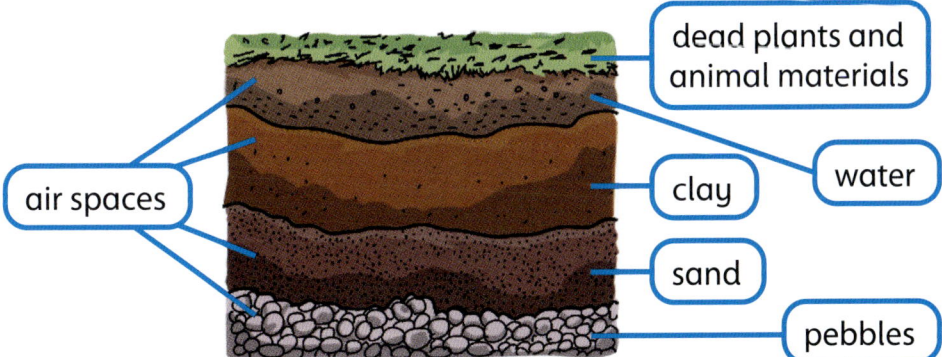

dead plants and animal materials

water

clay

air spaces

sand

pebbles

 Investigating different soils

You will be given four different soil samples to test.

1 Add five spoonfuls of each soil to its own jar of water.

2 Stir the mixtures and then let them settle.

What happens? Do any of the jars look like the one in the diagram below?

3 Draw and label your soil samples after they have settled.

4 Are the samples the same? How are they different?

Warning! Wash your hands after handling soil samples.

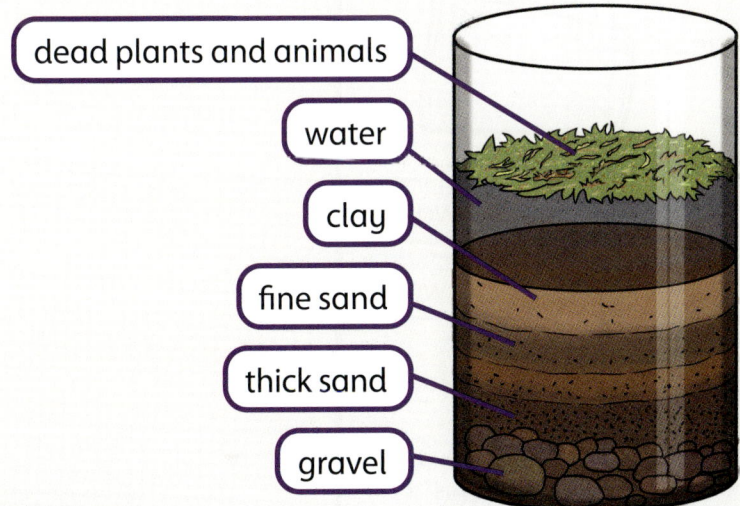

dead plants and animals

water

clay

fine sand

thick sand

gravel

 **Be a scientist**

Environmental scientists plan investigations to test soils to make sure they are safe to grow foods in.

▶ page 8

Key idea

Soil is important for life on Earth. Without it most plants would not grow.

■ For more activities, go to Workbook 3 page 41.

Types of soil

In this lesson you will recognise that there are different types of soil and some are better for growing plants than others.

Key words

chalky

clay

loam

sandy

If water does not run through soil easily, the soil can become too soft and muddy.

If water runs through soil too quickly, plants do not have time to take the water in.

Look at the photographs.

Which shows a soil that is too wet?

Which shows a soil that is too dry?

How well does your soil drain?

1 Make a funnel from a plastic bottle. Use the diagram to help you.

2 Add a small amount of cotton wool to the bottom of your funnel.

3 Put five spoonfuls of soil into the funnel.

4 Place the funnel into the top of a jar.

5 Slowly pour water onto the soil.

6 Use a stopwatch to time how long it takes for the water to pass through the soil and drain to in the jar.

Use the same test to compare your different soil samples.

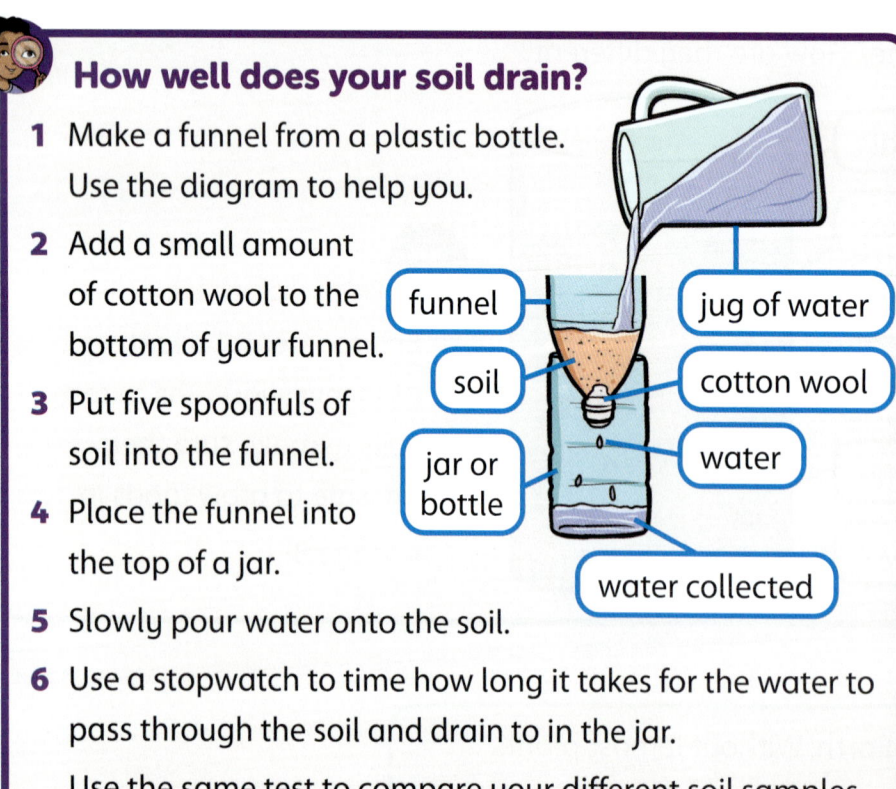

funnel

jug of water

soil

cotton wool

jar or bottle

water

water collected

■ For more activities, go to Workbook 3 page 42.

7 Which soil drained the quickest?

Which soil drained the slowest?

Be a scientist

Scientists collect data like this to check the drainage of soils. They can then share their results with others to prevent flooding.

▶ page 9

There are lots of different types of soil. Look at the table.

Chalky	Sandy
• Light brown with white pieces • Lots of holes, full of air • Water drains quickly	• A light colour • Lots of holes, full of air • Water drains quickly • Feels dry
Loam	**Clay**
• Dark brown • Ideal mixture of sand, clay and dead animals and plants • Water drains well • Full of the chemicals needed by plants	• Orange or grey • Very few holes, so not much air • Water drains slowly • Feels damp or wet

Which soil will get muddy after heavy rain?

Which soil will be too dry to grow crops?

Stretch zone

Group the soils you tested in your investigation into chalky, sandy, clay or loam soils.

Key idea

There are many types of soil. Some are better for growing plants than others.

Check how much you know.

Try the questions on pages 44–45.

■ For more activities, go to Workbook 3 page 43.

What have I learned about rocks and soil?

1 Circle any photographs that show rocks being used.

2 Label the layers of the Earth. Use the words in the word box.

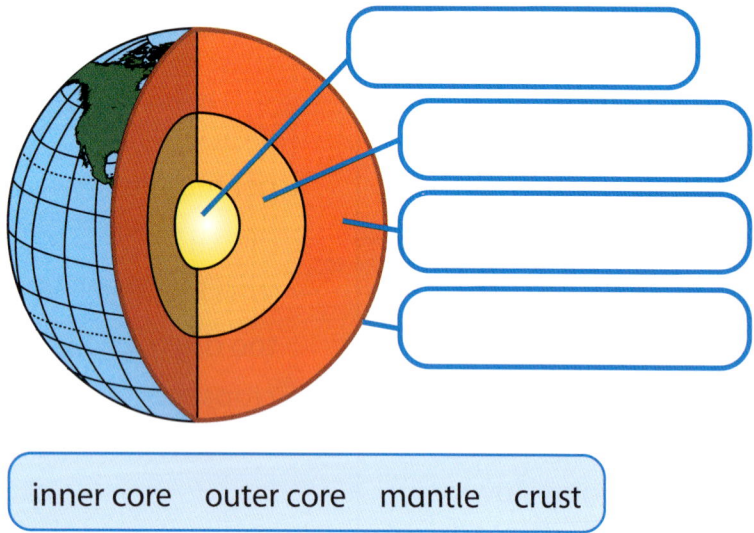

inner core   outer core   mantle   crust

3 Tick the type of rock formed when molten rock cools down slowly.

pebble ☐   mudstone ☐   igneous ☐

4 Tick the one word that is not part of the rock cycle.

erosion ☐

reflection ☐

melting ☐

sedimentary ☐

weathering ☐

44

■ For more activities, go to Workbook 3 page 44.

5 Label the layers found in soil. You can use the word box to help you.

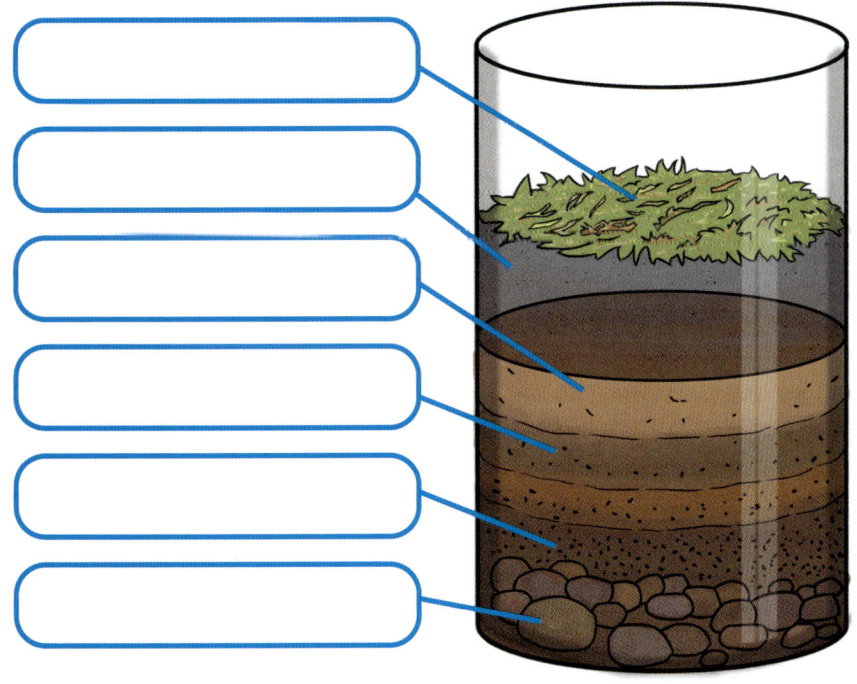

clay	dead plants and animals	fine sand	gravel	thick sand	water

6

This photograph is an example of a **fo**__ __ __ __. When **an**__ __ __ __ __ and plants

di__, they can be covered by mud and sand. The mud and sand turns into **ro**__ __ and

the **fo**__ __ __ __ is made.

7 Name three properties of rock that make it useful for building materials.

_____

_____

_____

■ For more activities, go to Workbook 3 page 45.

In this unit you will:

- identify and describe parts of flowering plants
- explore plant roots, leaves, stems, trunks and flowers
- find out that plants need water, light, air, nutrients from soil and space to grow
- investigate how water is taken in and moves through plants
- explore how temperature changes the way plants grow
- find out how flowers are involved in the life cycle of flowering plants.

dispersal flower growth
leaf nutrient pollen
pollination reproduce
root seed stem
transport trunk water

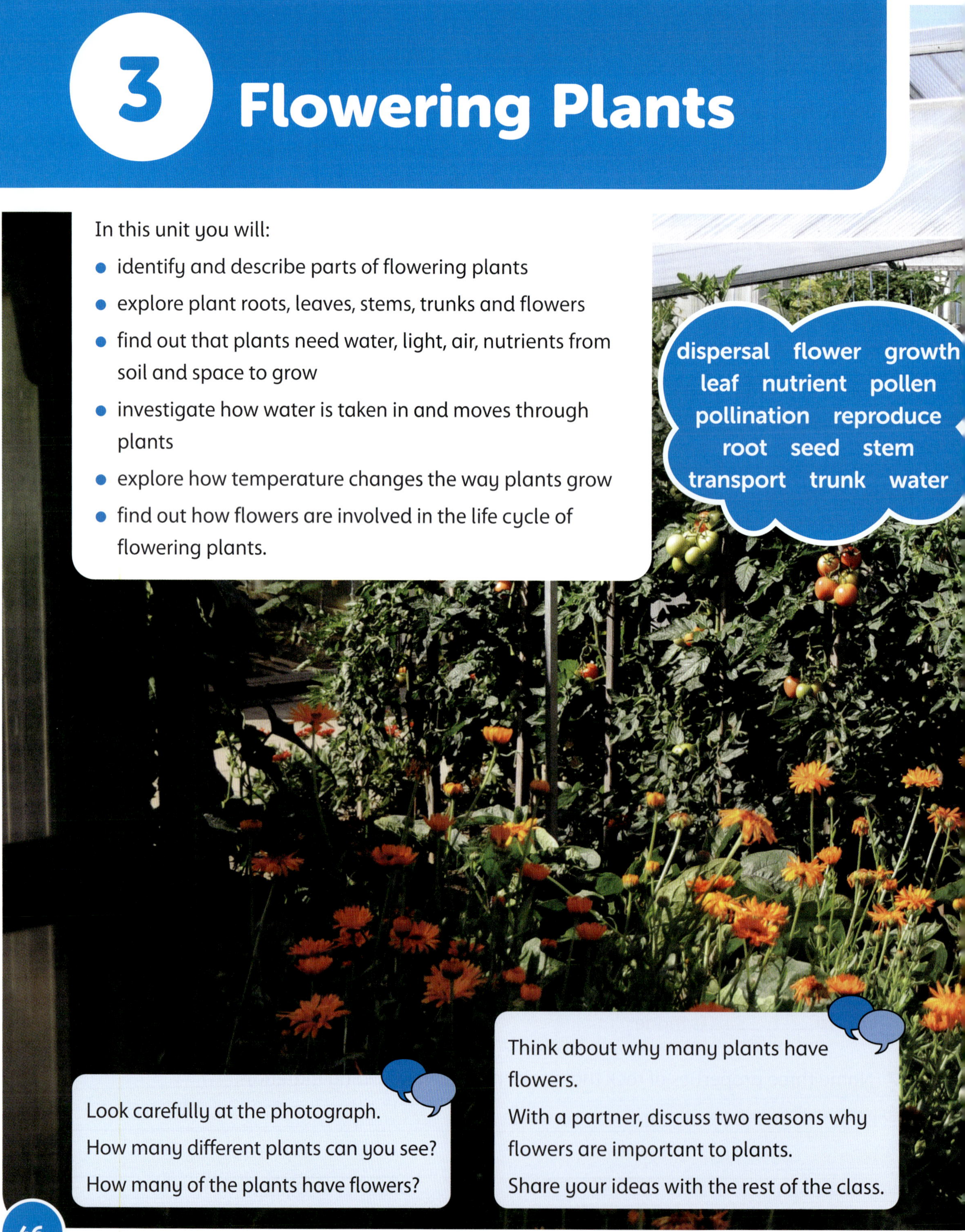

Look carefully at the photograph.

How many different plants can you see?

How many of the plants have flowers?

Think about why many plants have flowers.

With a partner, discuss two reasons why flowers are important to plants.

Share your ideas with the rest of the class.

Look at the fruits growing on the plants.

Have you seen these fruits before?

What are the fruits used for?

Science fact

Did you know that scientists have identified over 298 000 (two hundred and ninety eight thousand) species of plants?

■ For more activities, go to Workbook 3 pages 46–47.

Parts of a flowering plant

In this lesson you will explore that plants have roots, leaves, stems and flowers.

Key words

flower

leaf

root

stem

trunk

Think back

What do plants do, that animals also do?

How are plants and animals different?

The drawing shows the main parts of a flowering plant.

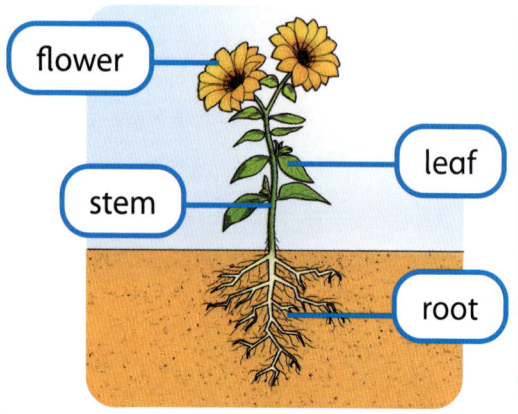

Look carefully at the photograph of the plant.

Can you identify the four main parts?

Be a scientist

Scientists make careful observations. They use drawings to record details. Drawings do not have to be an exact copy of something.

▶ page 9

Identifying plant parts

Your group will be given two different plants.

1 Carefully remove the plants from the pots.

2 Clean any soil from the plants.

3 Spread the plants out onto a piece of paper.

How are the plants similar? How are they different?

4 Identify the main parts of both plants.

5 Draw the plants and label the main parts.

Every part of a plant has a job to do. We say that each part has a function.

6 Read through the information in the table on the opposite page about the different parts of a flowering plant.

Use the information to add notes to your drawings of plants.

7 Display your labelled drawings to make a class gallery or exhibition.

■ For more activities, go to Workbook 3 page 48.

Read through the information in the table.

The columns have not been labelled. Decide which word from the word box should be used to label each column.

flower   stem   leaf   roots

Part of the plant				
What the part does	• In many plants this part has a nice colour and a nice smell. This attracts insects. • It is where seeds are produced.	• This part supports the plant. It keeps the plant upright. • It also transports water and food around the plant. • They can be flexible or woody. In trees, it is called a trunk.	• This part makes food for the plant from sunlight energy. • Scientists have a special name for this process. It is called photosynthesis.	• This part keeps the flowering plant anchored in the soil. • Some have tiny hairs on them to help them get water from the soil. • They are very important because plants need water to grow.

Stretch zone

Predict what would happen to a flowering plant if the stem was cut by a gardener by mistake.

Write down your plan. Tell your partner about it.

How could you investigate your ideas?

Key idea

Flowering plants have four main parts: flowers, stems, roots and leaves. In trees, the woody stem is called a trunk.

3 Flowering Plants

49

■ For more activities, go to Workbook 3 page 49.

Healthy and unhealthy plants

In this lesson you will observe the differences between healthy and unhealthy plants.

Key words

healthy/unhealthy

wilt

Plant A

Plant B

Look at the two plants in the photograph. Which plant would you describe as healthy? What clues did you use?

Scientists use their observation skills to give them clues about what is happening during an investigation. They write down what they see and may draw or take photographs.

Scientists also measure and count during their observations. They will then reach a conclusion about what has happened.

What would you measure and count if you were investigating the plants in the photograph?

Science fact

Scientists calculate that the Amazon rainforest produces half of Earth's oxygen. We need to keep it healthy.

When a plant does not get enough water, the leaves and stems are not as rigid. The plant's parts start to fall over. This is called wilting.

When a plant does not get enough nutrients from the soil or enough sunlight, its leaves might turn yellow or brown.

50

■ For more activities, go to Workbook 3 page 50.

Do some research to find out what is wrong with these plants. Discuss ideas about how the plants could be made healthy again.

Rescuing unhealthy plants

Imagine that you are a plant expert. Someone has brought you their unhealthy plants.

Your task is to investigate ways to make their plants healthy again.

1 Plan your investigations. When scientists plan an investigation they make sure it is a fair test. They change only one thing. Everything else is kept the same. Think about what you will change in your investigation.

2 Predict what you expect to find out.

3 Carry out the investigations.

4 Record your findings.

5 Present your findings as an information leaflet for gardeners showing them how to keep plants healthy.

Stretch zone

What might happen if a plant has too much sunlight or rain? Discuss your prediction with a partner.

Think about what the plant needs. How could this be added?

Were your predictions correct?

Key idea

Healthy plants have brighter flowers and leaves and stand more upright than unhealthy plants.

■ For more activities, go to Workbook 3 page 51.

Do plants need water?

In this lesson you will investigate whether plants need water to grow.

Think back

What does a plant look like when it has wilted?

With a partner, discuss why watering plants is important.

 Do plants need water to grow?

1 In your group choose two plants. Make sure the plants are the same size and same type. This is to make it a fair test.

2 Label one plant 'Water me'. Label the other plant 'Do not water me'.

3 Place your plants on a windowsill.

4 Predict what you expect to happen to each plant over the next few days.

5 Each day, give a little water to the plant labelled 'Water me'. Give no water to the other plant.

6 Copy and complete the table. Each day, write down what you see. These are your observations.

Day	Plant that has been watered	Plant that has NOT been watered
1	Plant looks healthy	Plant looks healthy
2		

7 Look at your observations. Do plants need water to grow well? This is your conclusion.

 **Be a scientist**
Remember to make your investigations fair. Your predictions should be based on things you already know.

▶ pages 7 and 8

52

■ For more activities, go to Workbook 3 page 52.

Once your observations are completed you can measure the length of each plant. This will give you more evidence about which plants are the most healthy.

Measuring plants

1 Take your plants out of the pots. Clean them so the roots are easy to see.

2 Measure the length of each plant. Do this three times.

Be a scientist

Scientists always measure things more than once. They then take an average. This makes their results more accurate.

▶ page 9

3 Write down your measurements and find the average. This means you add up the measurements for each plant and divide by three.

4 Record your results in a class table.

Was there any difference in the length of the watered plant and the unwatered plant?
What does this tell you about plants and water?

Stretch zone

Plan how you could show that plants lose water through their leaves.

Science fact

A large tree takes up over 350 litres of water from the soil every day. A lot of this is lost through the leaves.

Key idea

Without water, a plant will not be able to grow.

■ For more activities, go to Workbook 3 page 53.

Do plants need light?

In this lesson you will investigate whether plants need light to grow.

Key words

dark/light

photosynthesis

Think back

Discuss how you proved that plants need water for growth.

The grass is dying because it hasn't had any light

The grass is dying because the pot is too heavy and has squashed it.

With a partner, discuss these ideas. Whose idea do you agree with? Why?

You are going to plan an investigation to test the girl's idea.

Do plants need light to grow?

Light

No light

1 Choose six seedlings. Make sure they are the same size and type.

2 Plant three seedlings in a tray of soil. Make a label saying 'Light'. Put the tray on a windowsill.

3 Plant the other three seedlings in another tray. Make a label saying 'No light'. Put the tray in a dark place.

4 Give a little water to both sets of seedlings each day.

5 Predict what will happen to the seedlings over the next seven days.

6 Copy and complete the table. Each day write your observations.

Day	Seedlings with light	Seedlings with no light
1	Seedlings look healthy	Seedlings look healthy
2		

7 When you have collected all your observations, you can make a conclusion about whether plants need light to grow well. Present your findings as a poster or a computer presentation.

■ For more activities, go to Workbook 3 page 54.

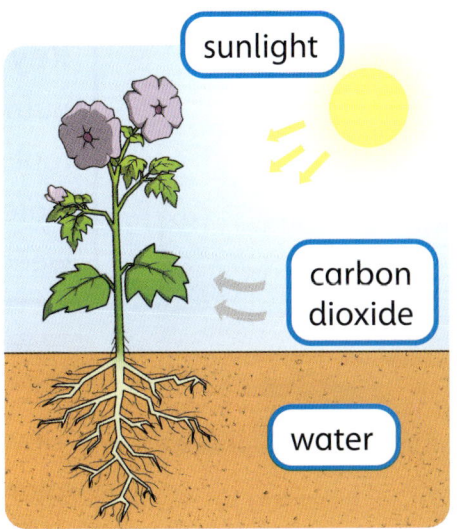

sunlight

carbon dioxide

water

How is the plant getting food?

What does this tell you about the importance of light to plants?

Plants and animals need food to grow and stay healthy.

Look at the diagram of the flowering plant. The leaves of a plant use the energy from the Sun in a special way to create food for the plant. This is called photosynthesis. For photosynthesis to happen the plant needs water from the ground. It also needs carbon dioxide. This comes from the air and from air spaces in the soil. Without air, a plant will not grow.

Planning a courtyard garden

Not all plants need the same amount of sunlight. Some grow in bright sunshine and others prefer more shady ground.

1 Your teacher will give you some seed packets. Read the seed packets to find out the amount of light each plant prefers.

2 Use this information to decide where in this courtyard each of the seeds should be planted.

3 Draw a plan of the courtyard and show where the plants will be placed.

Stretch zone

Predict which seeds will need the most watering. Explain your prediction.

partial shade

always in sunlight

always in shade

Key ideas

- Without light, a plant cannot grow.
- Different plants need different amounts of light.

3 Flowering Plants

55

The importance of roots

In this lesson you will investigate how roots hold the plant in place and allow it to take in water.

Key words

nutrients

root

water

weed

Think back

How does the plant get its water?

Weeds are plants that have grown where they are not wanted.

They can grow in paths or among other plants.

Weeds sometimes need to be removed but this isn't always easy.

Holding plants in place

You are going to go into the school grounds or local area to find some weeds.

1 Pull some of the weeds out. Try to find different types of weeds.

2 Write a table like this one in your book.

Warning! Wear gloves or a plastic bag over your hands.

Do not touch any plants until your teacher has checked them.

Weed	How easy to pull out of soil	Length of root in mm	How many branches in the root

3 Record how easy it was to pull the different plants out of the soil using this scale:

1 = pulled out easily   2 = difficult to pull out   3 = could not pull out

4 Look at the roots of each plant. Measure the length of the longest part of the root in millimetres. How many branches does the root have? Record the results in your table.

What does this investigation tell you about an important role of roots?

■ For more activities, go to Workbook 3 page 56.

Think back

Why do plants need water to reach the leaves?

What happens in the leaves? What is this process called?

Water and roots

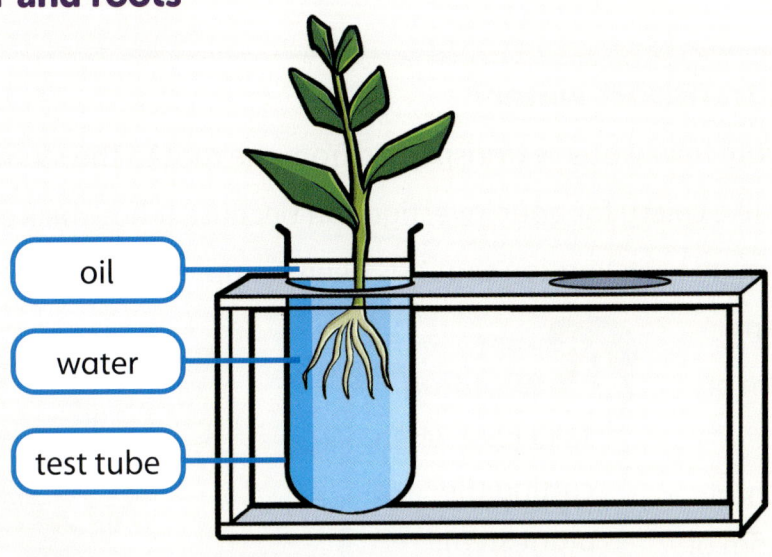

- oil
- water
- test tube

1 Set up a plant in a test tube as shown in the diagram.

2 Mark the level of the water with a marker pen.

3 Leave the plant in a warm and sunny place. Predict what will happen to the water level in the test tube.

4 Observe the plant every morning for three days. Mark the level of the water each time.

5 After three days write down your conclusions for your investigation.

Was your prediction correct? What does the investigation tell you about an important role of roots?

Some chemicals, called nutrients, that the plant needs to grow also enter through its roots. These nutrients, such as nitrates and phosphates, keep the plant healthy.

Stretch zone

Roots have small hairs on them. Research how these hairs increase the amount of water taken up. Make a poster to share your ideas.

Key idea

Roots spread out in the soil to anchor the plant and take in water and nutrients.

3 Flowering Plants

57

■ For more activities, go to Workbook 3 page 57.

The importance of stems

In this lesson you will investigate how water moves through plants.

Key words

stem

transport

water

How can we investigate how water travels through a plant?

How does a plant transport water?

You are going to investigate how water is transported from the root to the stem.

You will be using a plant like celery for your investigation because it has thick stems.

Look at this photograph of an investigation that has been set up.

1 Collect your celery stem.

2 Cut 2 cm off the bottom of the stem.

3 Pour water into the container until it covers the bottom of the stem.

4 Choose a food colouring. Add 10 drops of food colouring to the water.

 **Warning!**
Take care when cutting the plant stems. What could happen if you did not do this?

5 Stir the water and the food colouring very gently with the celery. Make sure that all the food colouring is mixed properly.

6 Put the container in a light place – perhaps on a windowsill.

Discuss what you think will happen to the plant. Predict how long you think it will take before you see anything happening.

7 Check your investigation over the next few days to see if there are any changes. Draw a picture to show what has happened.

■ For more activities, go to Workbook 3 page 58.

Stems contain special tubes. Some carry water from the roots to the rest of the plant. Others carry a sugary liquid food made in the leaves to the rest of the plant.

Flowers need to be high to attract insects, or in the wind to help spread pollen.

Leaves need to be in the Sun. They also need to be in the air so that gases can move in and out.

Study the drawing and the labels.
Why do flowering plants need stems to hold them upright?
What would happen if you laid a plant down on the soil?

Stretch zone

Do some research to find the difference between a stem, a branch and a trunk. Do they all move water from the roots? Present your ideas to a partner.

Key idea

Water is transported in plants from the roots through the stem to the leaves.

■ For more activities, go to Workbook 3 page 59.

Plant parts work together

In this lesson you will learn that plants need healthy roots, leaves and stems to grow well.

Key words

leaf

root

stem

Think back

We have carried out investigations which have shown us that plants need light, water and some chemical nutrients to grow well. When plants do not have these things, they become unhealthy.

Look at these two plants. Which plant is healthy? Which plant is unhealthy?

Roots need to spread out to find water. If they are squashed into a small pot they cannot do this.

When roots become squashed in a small pot we say the plant has become pot bound.

With a partner, discuss how you can help this plant to grow more healthily.

Agree two actions the owner of the plant can take to help their plant grow better.

■ For more activities, go to Workbook 3 page 60.

Are leaves needed to help roots?

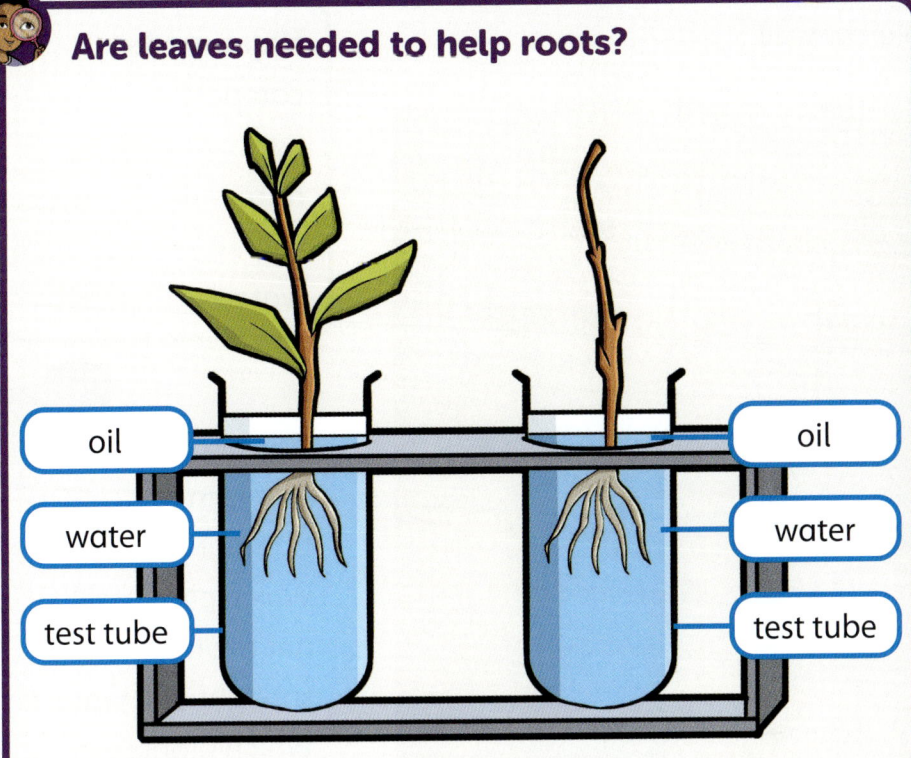

oil

water

test tube

oil

water

test tube

1 Set up the same investigation you used to investigate the role of roots. This time set up two plants.

2 Remove all of the leaves from one of the plants.

3 Mark the level of the water in both test tubes. Remember to cover the water level with oil.

4 Leave the plants in a sunny place.

5 Record the water level every day, for three days, for both plants.

What does this investigation tell you about the role of leaves in helping roots to take up water?

Stretch zone

Design an investigation to show whether healthy stems or healthy roots are needed for plants to grow well. Choose either stems or roots to investigate.

Carry out your investigation. Report your findings to the class.

Key idea

Plants need all of their major parts to be healthy to grow well. Every part has a job.

■ For more activities, go to Workbook 3 page 61.

Why plants need space to grow

In this lesson you will explore that plants need space so that roots, leaves and stems can grow well.

Key words

compost
light
nutrients
soil
water

Talk about the plants in the photograph. Which plants will get the most sunlight and water? Which plants will struggle to grow well?

Plants share water, sunlight and nutrients in the soil with other plants around them. They compete for these things.

What happens to crowded plants?

1 Plant out two sets of seeds into identical pots. Use the same amount and type of compost. Plant around three seeds, well spaced out, in one pot. Plant 20 seeds, crowded together, in the other.

2 Add the same volume of water to each pot so the compost is damp.

3 Place your pots in a warm place and observe them every day until seedlings appear.

4 Place the seedlings in a sunny place.

■ For more activities, go to Workbook 3 page 62.

5 Add the same volume of water to each pot every day so the compost does not dry out.

6 Observe the seedlings every day for 10 days. Measure the height of each seedling, its colour, and how many leaves it has.

Record your findings.

7 Uproot all of the plants and compare how healthy the leaves, stems and roots are. Measure the full length of each seedling, its colour, and how many roots it has.

Record your findings.

Which things were kept the same in your investigation to make this a fair test?

How well did the seedlings in each pot grow? Explain your findings.

Unfair competition

You are going to investigate how well a plant grows when it is planted beneath a larger plant.

1 Predict how well the small plant will grow.

2 Keep the plants watered.

3 Observe what happens to both plants for a few days.

Is the small plant able to compete for space, water and sunlight? Why?

 Stretch zone

Produce a short report that gives advice to gardeners and farmers about the need for plants to have their own space to grow in.

Key idea

Plants need space so they can grow well.

■ For more activities, go to Workbook 3 page 63.

Not too hot and not too cold!

In this lesson you will explore how temperature changes the way that plants grow.

Key words
adapted
temperature

Flowering plants grow best when the temperature is just right for them to grow.

Some plants like to grow in hot temperatures and some in very cold temperatures. Most plants like warm temperatures.

A plant that grows in hot temperatures cannot survive in very cold temperatures. A plant that grows in cold temperatures cannot survive in very hot temperatures. Plants are adapted to their habitats.

Look at the photographs of these plants and where they are growing. What do you notice? Do they look healthy?

Think back

Draw a plant that is adapted to live in a dry desert.

 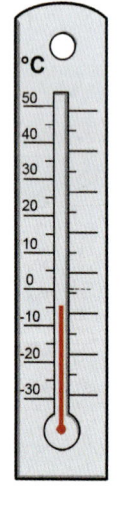

Discuss what has happened to this plant. Is the weather too cold or too hot for it?

In cold countries, greenhouses and polytunnels are used to grow vegetables, fruits and flowers. The air inside a greenhouse and polytunnel warms up quickly because hot air is trapped inside the glass or plastic. This means that plants which like warm weather can grow in the colder months.

■ For more activities, go to Workbook 3 page 64.

What happens to plants when it is too cold?

You will be given two identical plants.

1 Draw or take a photograph of your plants.

2 Place both in a warm and sunny place during the day.

3 At night, place one in a very cold place – a refrigerator or freezer is ideal.

   Do this for three days and three nights.

4 Now draw or take a photograph of the plants.

5 Compare both plants. Did the changes in temperature make any difference to how well the plants grew?

What does your investigation tell you about plant growth and temperature?

Stretch zone

Plan an investigation to find out what happens to plants when it is too hot. Share your plan with the class.

Researching plant habitats

Use books, magazines or the internet to find out how some plants are adapted to grow well in very hot places and some can survive in very cold places.

Design and make a plant scrap book to show these plants.

Key idea

Plants are adapted to grow best in temperatures that are just right for them.

Science fact

The movement of water out of the leaves helps to cool plants in hot weather.

■ For more activities, go to Workbook 3 page 65.

The life cycle of flowering plants

In this lesson you will explore the part that flowers play in the life cycle of flowering plants.

Think back

Plants can be grown from seeds.

Key words
anther
germination
pistil
reproduce
stamen
stigma

Living things do not live forever. They need to reproduce to make new versions of themselves.

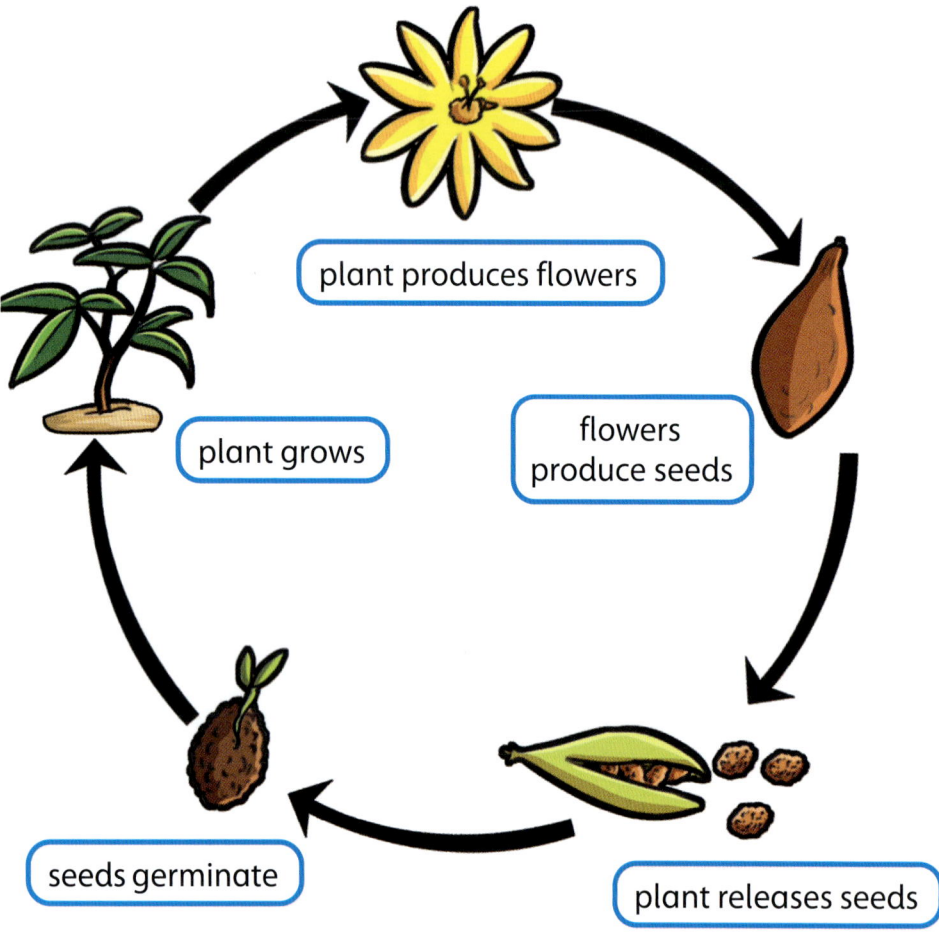

plant produces flowers

flowers produce seeds

plant grows

plant releases seeds

seeds germinate

Life cycle of a flowering plant

Discuss why flowering plants need to make seeds. What would happen if the seeds landed on concrete and not soil?

Reproduction in flowering plants takes place in the flower. Look at the diagram opposite. The female parts of a flower are called the carpel or pistil. The male parts of the flower are called the stamen.

The flower makes seeds. When seeds start to grow, they make small roots and stems. This is called germination.

What do pistils and stamens do? Why are seeds so important to flowering plants?

■ For more activities, go to Workbook 3 page 66.

Look at the diagram of the flower.

With your partner, name the parts that make up the pistil and the stamen.

Notice the other parts of the flower shown.

Be a scientist

Scientists respect the environment. They do not pick wild flowers to investigate. Why do you think this is?

▶ page 12

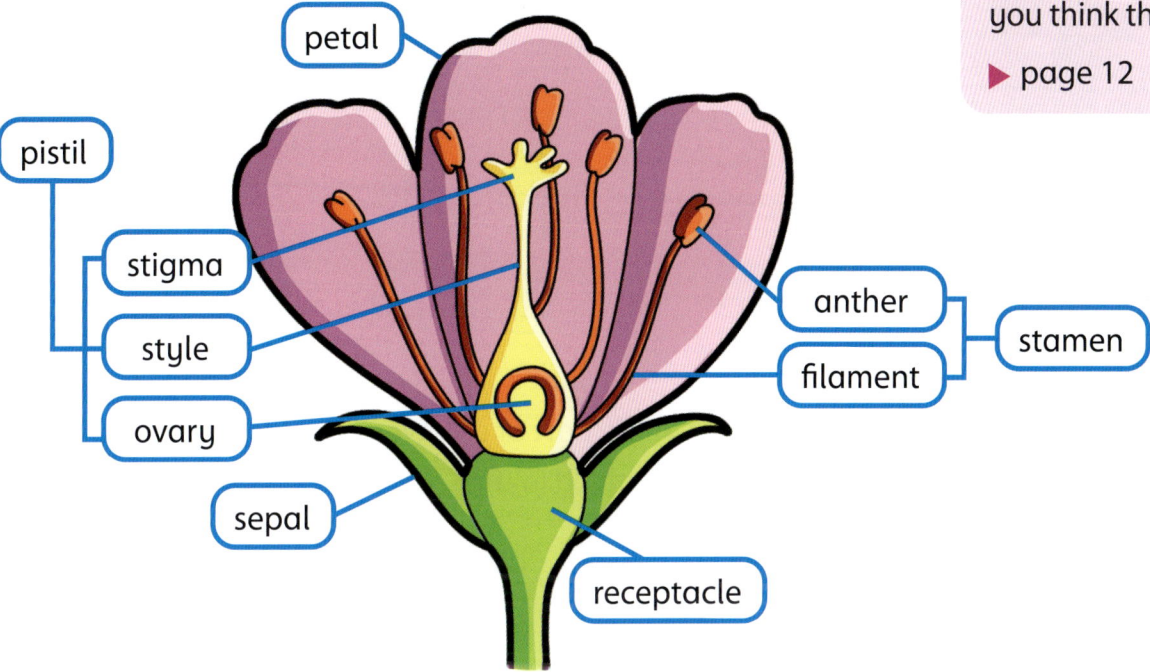

petal

pistil

stigma

style

ovary

sepal

receptacle

anther

filament

stamen

Exploring flowers

1 Collect two different flowers from your teacher.

2 Use a hand lens to look at all the parts.

3 Draw and label the two flowers. Use the diagram above to help you.

4 Write down how the two flowers are the same and how they are different.

Science fact

The largest flowers in the world are on a plant called *Rafflesia*. The flowers are up to a metre across.

Key ideas

- Flowering plants have a life cycle that starts with seeds. Seeds are made in the flower.
- All flowers have male and female parts.

■ For more activities, go to Workbook 3 page 67.

3 Flowering Plants

Pollination and seeds

In this lesson you will explore the part that pollination and seeds play in the life cycle of flowering plants.

Key words

agent

pollen

pollination

pollinator

seed

Look at the photograph. What is covering the bee's legs? What attracts the bee to the flower?

Pollination

Pollination is the transfer of pollen from the male part of a flower to the female part of a flower. If an insect is involved in this pollen transfer, it is called a pollinator.

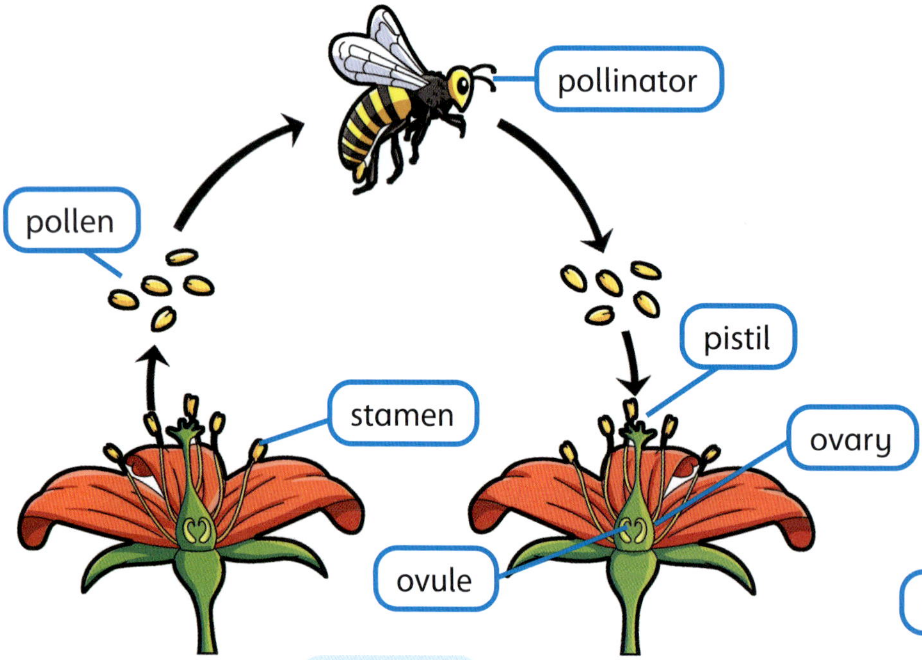

pollinator

pollen

pistil

stamen

ovary

ovule

Pollination

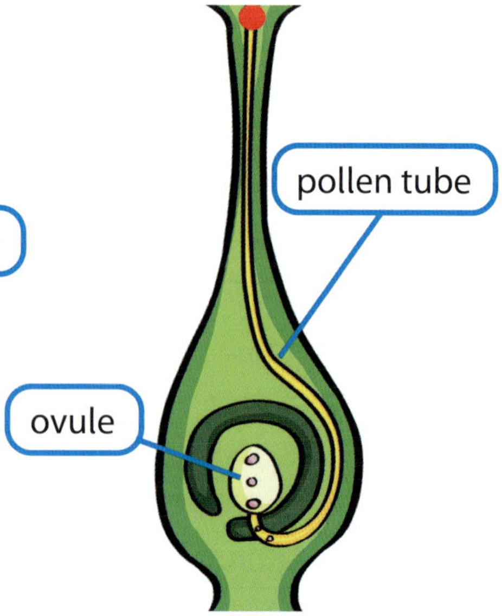

pollen tube

ovule

Fertilisation

After pollination, the pollen grows down to the ovary and joins with an ovule. This is called fertilisation. The ovule changes to make a seed.

68

■ For more activities, go to Workbook 3 page 68.

Observing a plant pistil

1 Take a flower and lay it out on your table.

2 Use a hand lens to find the pistil.

3 Gently cut the pistil out of the flower with some scissors.

4 Cut down the middle of the pistil and open it up.

5 Draw what you see. Label the stigma, style, ovary and any ovules.

Warning! Take care with scissors. Do not move around the room with them. Discuss why this is important.

Seeds

Once seeds have formed, they need to be spread or dispersed. This can happen in a number of ways.

blown in the wind

carried in water

sticking to animals

being eaten by animals

bursting or exploding

Discuss some examples of seed dispersal that you have seen in your area.

Seeds need to be dispersed so that the new plants do not need to compete with the parent plants for water, nutrients, air, light and space. This will give them a better chance of survival.

Check how much you know.
Try the questions on pages 70–71.

Key ideas

- After fertilisation, seeds form.
- Seeds disperse in different ways.

3 Flowering Plants

69

■ For more activities, go to Workbook 3 page 69.

1 Label the four parts of a flowering plant. Use the words in the word box.

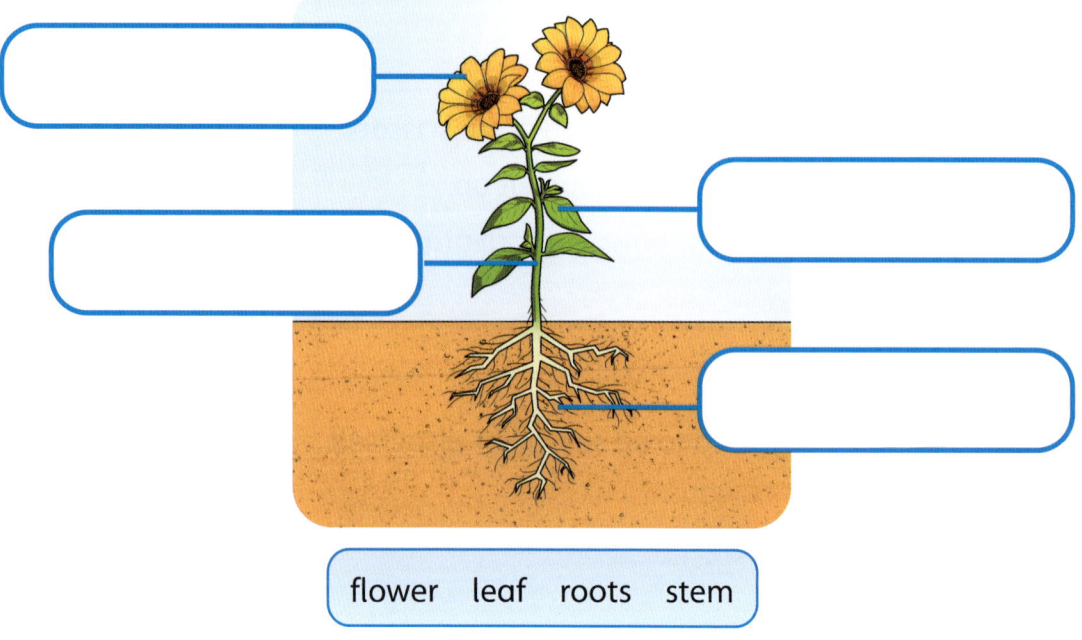

flower   leaf   roots   stem

2 Put the life cycle of a flowering plant in the correct order. Write the letters in the boxes below. The first one has been done for you.

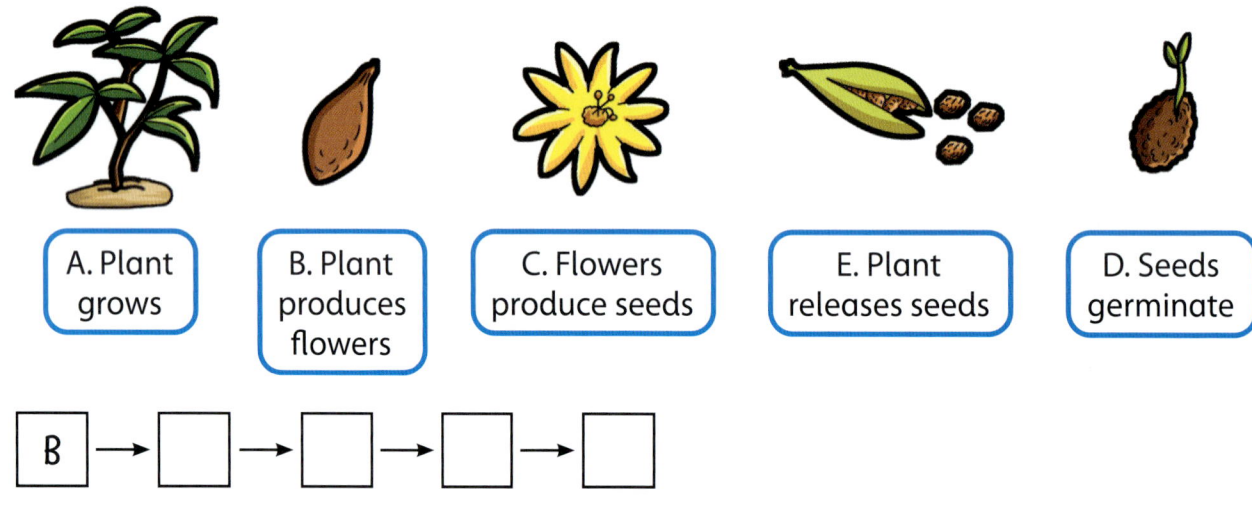

A. Plant grows   B. Plant produces flowers   C. Flowers produce seeds   E. Plant releases seeds   D. Seeds germinate

B → ☐ → ☐ → ☐ → ☐

3 Name five things that a plant needs to grow. The first letter of each word will help you.

l __ __ __ __   s __ __ __

w__ __ __ __   n __ __ __ __ __ __ __ __

a __ __

■ For more activities, go to Workbook 3 page 70.

4 **a** Draw arrows on the picture to show the route that water takes to enter and move around a plant.

   b What other function does a root have?

   _____

5 Label the diagram to show how pollen can move from one plant to another. Use the words from the word box.

| ovary   ovule   pollen   pollinator   pistil   stamen |

6 Study the table below. It shows the height of seedlings grown in different conditions.

Conditions	Height of the seedlings (centimetres)			
	Measure 1	Measure 2	Measure 3	Average
Light and air but no water	3	2	4	3
Light, water and air	7	7	9	8

   a Why did the scientist measure the seedlings three times?

   _____

   _____

   b What do the results tell you about what seedlings need to grow healthily?

   _____

   _____

■ For more activities, go to Workbook 3 page 71.

4 Introducing Forces and Magnets

In this unit you will:

- revise that pushes and pulls are examples of forces
- explore how forces can make objects move or stop
- understand that some forces need contact between two objects but magnetic forces act at a distance
- find out about magnets and magnetic force.

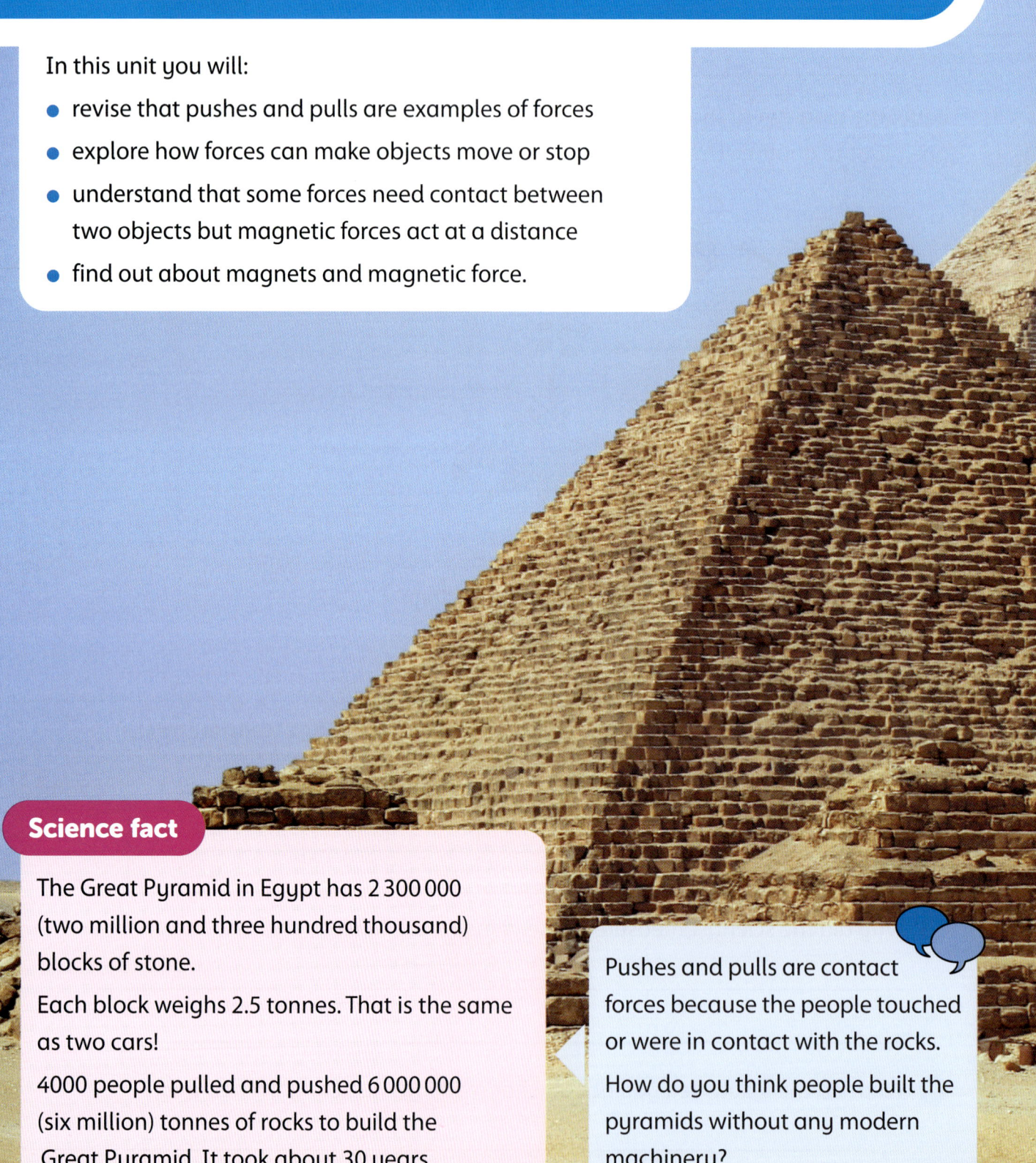

Science fact

The Great Pyramid in Egypt has 2 300 000 (two million and three hundred thousand) blocks of stone.

Each block weighs 2.5 tonnes. That is the same as two cars!

4000 people pulled and pushed 6 000 000 (six million) tonnes of rocks to build the Great Pyramid. It took about 30 years.

Pushes and pulls are contact forces because the people touched or were in contact with the rocks.

How do you think people built the pyramids without any modern machinery?

attract   contact force
force   friction   magnet
non-contact force
pole   pull   push
repel

The Earth's magnetic field force protects us from the Sun. When solar rays hit the magnetic field it causes magnetic storms like the Northern lights.

What do you know about magnets?

Have you seen or used a magnet today?

N   S

■ For more activities, go to Workbook 3 pages 72–73.

Pushes and pulls

In this lesson you will revise that pushes and pulls are examples of forces.

Key words
direction
force
pull/push

Think back

Have you pushed or pulled something today?
Think about when you got dressed this morning. You might have pushed your hand into a sleeve and pulled the sleeve up your arm.

Pushes and pulls are examples of forces.

- A push usually makes an object move away from you.
- A pull usually moves an object towards you.

What are the small boats doing?

Look at these photographs with a partner. Discuss the questions. Decide whether pushes or pulls are being shown.

What is this child doing?

74

We can use arrows to show the direction of a force.

If an object is moving to the right, then the force must be acting to the right and we can draw an arrow to the right. A force can go in any direction.

Some push and pull forces are very small and some are very big.

A butterfly lands on a plant with a very small force. We would not be able to feel it.

The photograph below shows a road has been damaged by a big earthquake. The push and pull forces of the earthquake were very strong.

What force is stopping the trolley from rolling away?

Surveying pushes and pulls

Work with a partner for this investigation.

1 Look around the room. Can you see anyone using a push or a pull force? Record your observations.

2 Think about three examples where you have used a push or a pull force today. With your partner, choose one of your examples and draw a diagram. Add arrows to show the direction of the forces.

Was the force you chose a big force or a small force? How do you know?

Why is it important to be able to measure forces?

Key ideas

- Pushes and pulls are forces.
- The direction of a force is shown with an arrow.

■ For more activities, go to Workbook 3 page 75.

Measuring pushes and pulls

In this lesson you will find out that we can measure forces with forcemeters.

Think back

What force do we use to open a door?

We can measure the amount of force using an instrument called a forcemeter.

Key words

force

forcemeter

gravity

newtons

weight

How does a forcemeter work?

You are going to use a forcemeter.

1 Your teacher will give you objects of different sizes.

2 Attach each object to the forcemeter, one at a time.

3 Notice where the pointer reaches on the forcemeter.

4 Put the objects in order of how far they made the pointer go down. What do you notice?

5 Look at the forcemeters **a** and **b** and find 'NEWTONS' and the scale. Some forcemeters also show the mass in kilograms or grams.

Work out the force in newtons and the mass in grams shown on the two scales.

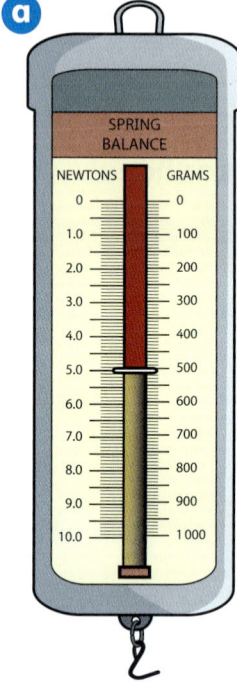

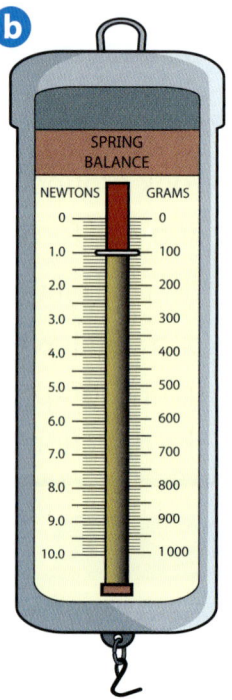

Weight is a force and it is measured in newtons. The symbol for newtons is N. The weight of an object is how much it is pulled down to the Earth by gravity. The greater the mass of an object (how much of it there is), the greater the gravitational force.

Mass is measured in grams (g) and kilograms (kg). The greater the mass of an object, the greater its weight will be.

■ For more activities, go to Workbook 3 page 76.

How much force is needed to open a door?

1 Attach the hook on the forcemeter to the door handle of a slightly open door.

2 Hold the other end of the forcemeter and pull.

3 Look at the forcemeter to see how far the needle goes down. Read the amount if you can.

4 How much pulling force did you need to open the door?

5 Investigate other doors.

Now copy and complete the table.

Location of the door	Force (N)

What did you find out from your investigation?
What force is needed to open a door?

Be a scientist

Scientists repeat their measurements to make sure they have not made a mistake.

▶ page 9

Some forcemeters can measure a push force as well as a pull force.

Try to push your book across the table. Now pull the book across the table.

Was the amount of force the same when pushing or pulling your book?

Science fact

An astronaut on the Moon weighs less than on Earth even though the astronaut's mass is the same. This is because the gravitational pull on the Earth is six times more than on the Moon.

Key idea

We can measure forces using a forcemeter.

■ For more activities, go to Workbook 3 page 77.

Making shapes with forces

In this lesson you will explore how forces can change the shape of objects.

Key words
force
pull/push

Forces can change the shape of objects. This can be very useful.

Look at what the people are doing in the photos. They are using a push or a pull to make objects we can use and eat.

A push

B push and pull

C push and pull

Crumple a piece of paper into the smallest ball that you can.

What force have you used to do this?

■ For more activities, go to Workbook 3 page 78.

Using forces to change the shape of modelling clay

1 Use a wooden or plastic hammer to see what shape you can make out of a lump of clay. Work gently.

2 Use your hands to make a pot out of a lump of clay.

3 Use your hands to push and pull the clay to make a flat pizza shape.

4 Draw 'before' and 'after' pictures of each of your models. You could take pictures or video to record your investigation.

5 Display your results and ask others to compare their investigation with yours.

The force of push is used to make parts for cars and planes. Machines press metal into moulds. They use the pushing force to create shapes from the flat metal.

Using forces to mould modelling clay

1 Press modelling clay into different moulds.

2 Take the clay out of the moulds.

What forces did you use to make the moulds?

Stretch zone

Plan a method to measure the force needed to roll out modelling clay. You could use the following questions to help you:

● What equipment would you use?

● What unit of measurement would you use?

Key idea

Forces can change the shape of an object.

■ For more activities, go to Workbook 3 page 79.

Forces can stop or start things moving

In this lesson you will explore how forces can make objects start or stop moving.

Key words
force
start/stop

Forces make things go faster and slow down or stop.

When is it useful to make an object stop?

Using forces to start and stop a toy car

Use a toy car to investigate how forces make the car change speed and stop.

1 Gently push a toy car along a smooth, flat surface such as the classroom floor.

2 Observe how the car moves.

3 Measure how far the car travels before it stops. Record the distance your car travelled in cm.

4 Now try to stop the car before it stops itself.

Warning! Be careful not to trip over objects on the floor when moving around.

How did you start and stop the car?

■ For more activities, go to Workbook 3 page 80.

Changing the speed and direction of a toy car

1 Now push the car as hard as you can along the classroom floor. Make sure nobody is in front of the car.

2 Observe the speed the car travelled.

3 Measure how far it travelled.

4 Record the distance.

5 Push your car again. This time try to make it change direction on its journey.

> How did you make the car move faster?
> How did you make it change direction?

The more force there is, the faster and further the car goes.

The less force there is, the slower the car goes.

 Stretch zone

How do you measure the speed that a car travels?

What other information would you need? Hint: speed is the distance an object travels in a set time, such as a second, a minute or an hour.

Key idea

Forces can make an object start or stop moving.

■ For more activities, go to Workbook 3 page 81.

Forces on different surfaces

In this lesson you will explore how forces can make objects move faster or slower.

Key words

fast/slow

ramp

start/stop

Think back

What makes things go faster?

How fast things can go and how quickly they can stop also depends on the surface they are travelling along.

How fast do you think the vehicle in this photograph can go?
What is stopping it from going faster?

How well do things move on different surfaces?

We can investigate how things travel along different surfaces using a ramp and different materials.

1 Make a ramp out of strong cardboard or another firm material.

2 Put some books or a box on the floor and lean the ramp against them.

3 Hold your car at the top of the ramp and let go.

4 Put the ramp on surfaces made of different materials, such as soil, concrete and carpet. Measure how far the toy car travels on each surface.

5 Copy and complete the table.

Type of surface	Distance travelled (cm)	Observations

Which surface made the car travel the fastest?
Which surface made the car travel the furthest?

82

■ For more activities, go to Workbook 3 page 82.

Comparing the movement of different items on different surfaces

You are going to compare how different items move on different surfaces.

1 Try rolling a ball down the same ramp onto the different surfaces.

2 Record your results in a table like in the last investigation.

3 Compare your findings about the car and the ball.

> Does the ball travel faster than the car or more slowly?
>
> Do the different surfaces make the ball behave in the same way as the car?
>
> Do the objects go faster on a smooth or a rough surface?

4 Now work with a partner to investigate the following questions. These will help you conclude your investigations.

- What happens to the toy car if you push it instead of just letting it go?
- What happens to the toy car when you push it very hard?

Be a scientist

Remember, scientists only alter one thing in an investigation to make it a fair test.

▶ page 8

Stretch zone

Why does the rough surface make the car move more slowly? Discuss your ideas with a partner.

Key ideas

- Forces can make objects move faster or slower.
- Different surfaces affect how fast or slowly objects move across them.

■ For more activities, go to Workbook 3 page 83.

Friction

In this lesson you will explore how a contact force called friction can affect the speed of moving objects.

Key words

contact force

friction

grip

Think back

With a partner, talk about what we have learned about surfaces. What kind of surface is best for a children's slide?

Some surfaces help objects to travel quickly. This is very useful if you are making a slide or you want to go ice skating.

Some surfaces help objects to travel more slowly. This is useful if you want cars to go more slowly, as we found out on page 82.

Rubbing surfaces together

1 Put your hands palm down on the surface of your desk and press down lightly. Move your hands lightly across the desk.

2 Now press your hands firmly down on the desk and move them across the desk.

Did you feel a dragging feeling? Was this more or less when you pressed down firmly on the desk? What do you think is causing the dragging feeling?

The dragging you felt is called friction. Friction is a force that always happens when two surfaces rub together.

Some forces, like friction, need contact between the surfaces of objects. These are called contact forces. Other forces do not need to make contact to work on the object. These are non-contact forces.

Look again at the photographs of the ice skaters above and the vehicle on a rough surface on page 82. Which surface do you think causes the most friction?

■ For more activities, go to Workbook 3 page 84.

When two surfaces rub together, friction causes them to grip.

Some shoes have good grip to stop us falling on slippery ground. Walkers have good grip on their boots to stop them slipping.

With your partner, name two groups of people who wear shoes with a good grip.

Look at the pictures of different shoes. Point to the ones you think have the best grip.

Brakes use friction to stop or slow down moving things.

When you press the brake lever on a bike, the brake blocks squeeze against the bike wheel, stopping the bike wheel from moving.

Do you have brakes on your bike? When do you use them? What do they do?

Stretch zone

Can you explain your ideas about your choice of shoes with the best grip?

Think of an investigation you could do to test which shoe has the best grip.

Write or draw a picture explaining what you would do.

Key ideas

- Friction is a force that happens when two surfaces rub together.
- Friction is a contact force that gives us grip and slows things down.

4 Introducing Forces and Magnets

85

■ For more activities, go to Workbook 3 page 85.

Forces can change the direction of moving objects

In this lesson you will explore how forces can make moving objects change direction.

Key words
direction
friction
movement

Think back

When you throw a ball at a wall, what force makes the ball go forward?

What do you think will happen to the ball when it hits the wall? Discuss your ideas with a partner.

What happens when a moving object hits another object?

1 Sit on the floor in front of a wall or door. Carefully roll the ball towards the wall. What happens?

2 Now sit opposite a partner. Both roll a ball towards each other so the balls hit. What happens?

3 Try this with toy cars. What happens?

4 Copy out the table below and use this to record what you found.

Experiment	What happened?
Ball rolled to a wall	
Two balls rolled towards each other	
Two toy cars pushed towards each other	

■ For more activities, go to Workbook 3 page 86.

Footballers push the ball when they kick it. Footballers can use forces to decide where they want to kick a ball.

They make decisions about how fast the ball is coming towards them, what angle it is coming at, and how much spin it has.

Playing bowls

Work with a small group or partner for this activity.

1 Set up six bottles near a wall. These are your skittles. Follow the pattern you see in the picture. Now stand three metres away from the skittles.

2 Take it in turns to roll the ball towards the skittles. Try to knock them all over.

3 Remove any skittles that have fallen.

4 Count how many times you have to roll the ball before all of the skittles have been knocked over.

5 When everyone has had a turn, find out who needed the least number of rolls.

With your group, discuss these questions:
How did you use forces in your bowls game?
How did forces change the speed and direction of the ball?
How did forces affect the skittles?

Stretch zone

Think about other examples of sports that use forces. Draw one example of a sport and label where the player or players are using pushes and pulls.

Key idea

Forces can make moving objects change direction.

■ For more activities, go to Workbook 3 page 87.

Is it magnetic?

In this lesson you will find out that some materials are magnetic, but many are not.

Key words
attract/repel
magnet
magnetic
non-contact force
pole
push/pull

Some metals have a very important property. They can be made into magnets. Magnets pull some materials towards them. We say that they attract other materials.

This happens because of the force of magnetism. This force does not need contact between objects. It is a non-contact force.

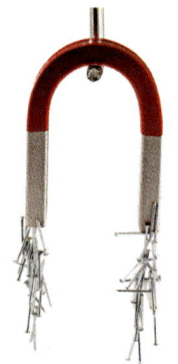

human-made magnet

natural magnet - lodestone

Look at the photographs. What is happening to the tacks and paper-clips?
Can you describe it to your partner?

Some materials are natural magnets. A rock called lodestone is a magnet.

Other magnets are human made.

Are all materials magnetic?

1 Use a magnet to test the objects your teacher gives you.
- If an object is attracted towards the magnet, the object is made of a magnetic material.
- If an object is not attracted towards the magnet, the object is made of a non-magnetic material.
2 Design a table to record your results.

Can you see a pattern in your results? What type of materials are magnetic?

You may have found out that non-metals are non-magnetic. Some examples of non-metals are wood, plastic and ceramic.

Some metals are magnetic. Iron, steel, nickel and cobalt are magnetic.

Other metals are non-magnetic. Some non-magnetic metals are gold, silver, copper and aluminium.

Close this book. Can you name two magnetic materials? Can you name two non-magnetic materials?

■ For more activities, go to Workbook 3 page 88.

Magnets have two ends called poles. One end of a magnet is the North-seeking pole. The other end is the South-seeking pole. You will learn more about magnetic poles in a later lesson.

What happens when we bring two magnets together?

1   Slowly push two magnets together with the poles labelled N facing each other.

    What do you feel?

2   Push the magnets together with the poles labelled S facing each other.

    What do you feel?

3   Push the magnets together with an S-pole facing an N-pole.

    What do you feel?

You have discovered a scientific law. This is the law of magnetism.

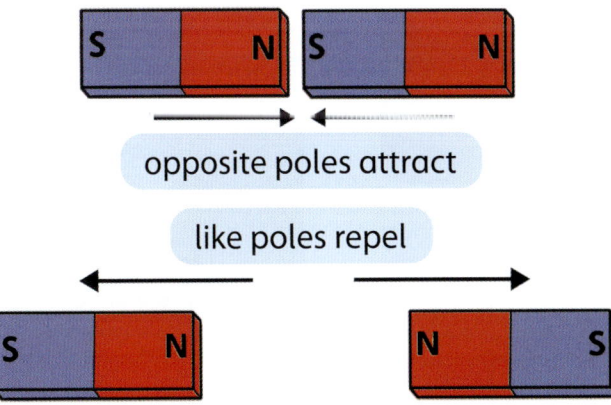

opposite poles attract

like poles repel

If the poles pull together, they are attracted. If the poles push apart, they are repelled.

Key ideas

- Magnetism is a non-contact force.
- Magnets can pull or attract some materials towards them. They can also push or repel some materials away from them.

■ For more activities, go to Workbook 3 page 89.

Using magnets

In this lesson you will explore some of the uses and strength of magnets.

Magnets have many uses. When they attract magnetic materials very powerfully we say they have a high magnetic strength. Some magnets have a high magnetic strength and others have a low magnetic strength.

Key words

magnet

strength

This scrap car is being lifted by a magnet

This Maglev train is not touching the track because giant magnets are holding it above the railway

Magnets are holding the notes in place on this refrigerator door

Science fact

Scientists have discovered the most powerful magnet in the universe. It is a star found in deep space called Magnetar.

Make a fridge magnet

1 Your teacher will help you make a fridge magnet.
2 Test to find out how many sheets of paper your fridge magnet can hold without falling off.

Warning!

Magnets can cause damage to computers and smartphones. Never put a magnet near these devices.

■ For more activities, go to Workbook 3 page 90.

You can use magnets to make games and puzzles.

 Are all magnets the same strength?

Work with a partner for this investigation.

Your teacher will give you different magnets to test.

1 Try to pick up paperclips with each of the magnets. Add more paperclips end-to-end so you have a paperclip chain.

2 Record how many paperclips each magnet can pick up. The more paperclips that can be picked up, the stronger the magnet.

3 Do your results show if all magnets are the same strength?

Why is it important that you use the same size of paperclip for each test?

 Design and make a magnetic game

1 Plan and then make your game. Give it a creative name.

2 Invite another group to try your game.

3 Put your games on display. Look at all the games carefully.

4 Write the name of the game you think is the best. You cannot choose your own game.

Write a reason why you think the game is the best.

5 Your teacher will tell you which game is the class favourite. Do not worry if your game does not win. How can you make your game better?

 Be a scientist

Scientists always think about how to improve their investigations. Some of the greatest inventions in the world did not work first time.

▶ page 13

 Stretch zone

Explain how your game works. Use the key words to help you.

Key ideas

- Magnets are used in everyday life.
- Magnets have different magnetic strengths.

■ For more activities, go to Workbook 3 page 91.

Magnets have poles

In this lesson you will investigate the poles of magnets.

Think back

Magnets have two ends called poles. One end is the North pole and the other end is the South pole.

Magnetism is an invisible force of attraction between some metals. The magnetic force comes from the billions of tiny particles called atoms that make up the metal. Each atom is like a very tiny magnet.

Talk with your partner about magnets. Each of you should say one thing that magnets do.

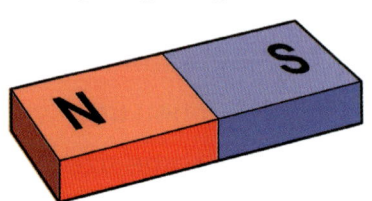

In non-magnetic metals all the tiny magnetic atoms point in different directions.

In magnetic metals all the North ends of the tiny magnetic atoms point North and all the South ends point South. When the atoms are lined up, an invisible magnetic force appears.

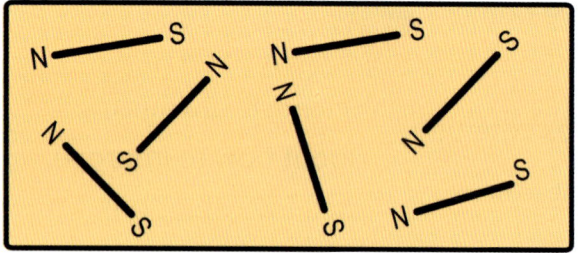

Non-magnetic metal

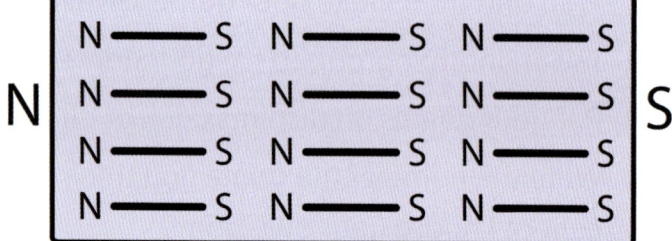

Magnetic metal

Magnet survey

You are going to survey your school for how magnets are used.

1 Look around the school for uses of magnets.

2 Write down any uses of magnets that you see.

3 Design a poster to tell people about the uses of magnets you found.

■ For more activities, go to Workbook 3 page 92.

Why does the Earth have a North Pole and a South Pole?

At the centre of the Earth there is a liquid core. The core is made of molten metals that are magnetic. It creates a massive magnetic pulling force at each end. This force wraps around the Earth's surface and creates the Earth's magnetic field with a North end and a South end.

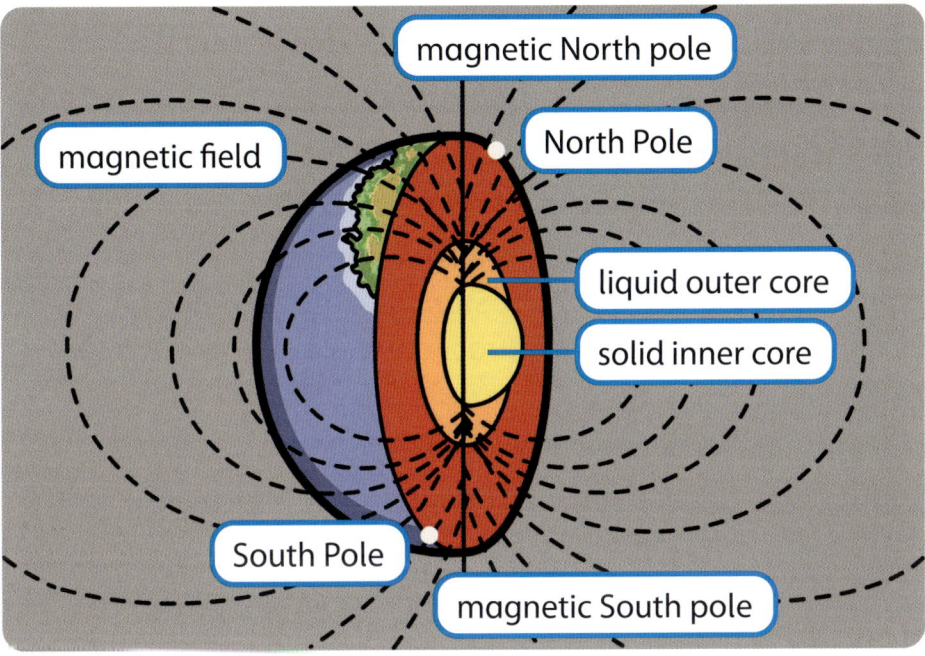

The North end of a bar magnet is attracted to the North Pole. The South end of a bar magnet is attracted to the South Pole.

What is a compass?

A compass is a magnet that can turn freely so it always lies in a North to South direction.

Magnets can help us find the North and South poles.

When is it helpful to have a compass? How does a compass help us find our way?

Key idea

Magnets have a North pole and a South pole.

Stretch zone

Write a short information page that explains to people why magnets have a North and a South pole.

4 Introducing Forces and Magnets

93

■ For more activities, go to Workbook 3 page 93.

Investigating the poles of a magnet

In this lesson you will investigate how magnets attract and repel each other.

We are going to investigate what happens when we bring two magnets together.

What do you predict will happen?

Key words

attract/repel

bar magnet

North/South

pole

How do magnets react together?

You will need two bar magnets. Make sure one end is labelled North (N) and the other end South (S).

1 Look at diagrams **A** to **E**, each showing two magnets. Start with your magnets in these positions and think about whether they will attract or repel each other. Write your prediction for each diagram.

2 Slowly bring the two magnets together as shown in each diagram.

Observe the magnets. Do they pull together (attract) or push apart (repel)?

Record your observations for each diagram.

A South end facing North end	**B** North end facing North end	**C** South end facing South end

 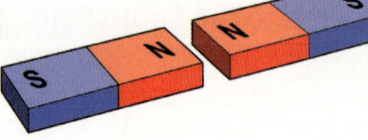 

D North end above North end and South end above South end	**E** South end above North end and North end above South end

3 Look at all of your results. What does your investigation tell you about how magnets attract and repel each other?

4 Write a conclusion about how magnets react together.

■ For more activities, go to Workbook 3 page 94.

Remember: The law of magnetism is: 'Opposite poles attract and like poles repel.'

Did your investigations show you this?

The magnetic forces on Earth come out near the North Pole and the South Pole. These two forces are attracted to each other. They bend around the Earth's surface to meet in the middle.

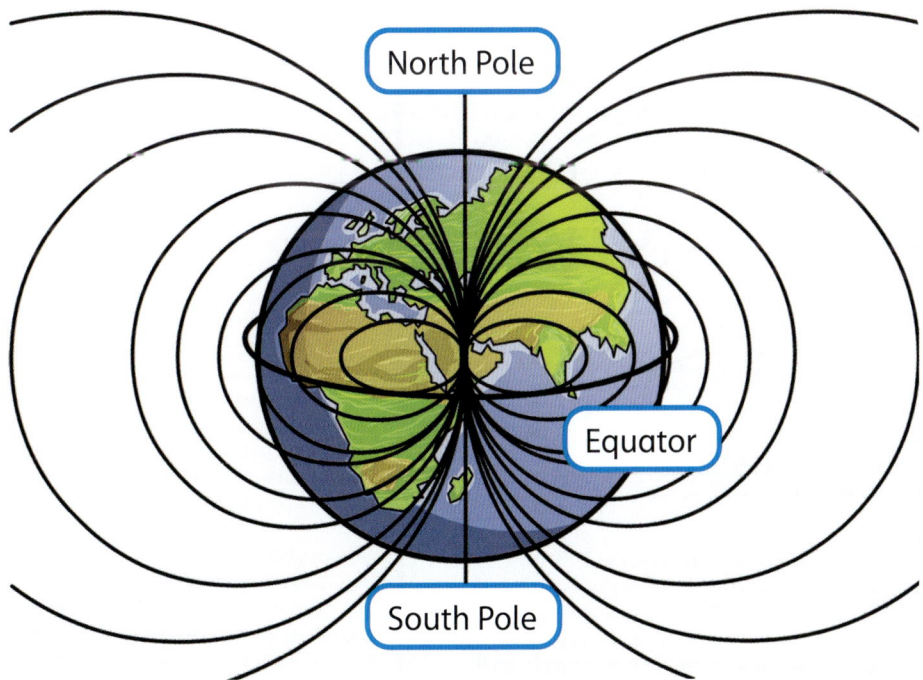

North Pole

Equator

South Pole

Stretch zone

Where do you think the magnetic field is the strongest, at the Poles or at the Equator?

Key ideas

- Opposite poles of a magnet attract each other.
- Like poles repel each other.

4 Introducing Forces and Magnets

■ For more activities, go to Workbook 3 page 95.

Which materials are magnetic?

In this lesson you will find out which materials are magnetic.

The Earth's core is magnetic. It is made of three metals: iron, nickel and cobalt. Iron, nickel and cobalt are the only magnetic metals. Iron is very common on the Earth's surface and nickel is quite common but expensive. Cobalt is extremely rare.

Steel is a mixture of metals. Other metals, such as nickel and chromium, can be added to it to make it stronger. Metals mixed together are called alloys.

Not all steel objects are magnets. They only behave like a magnet when they are magnetised.

Remember: to be a magnet, all the tiny Norths and Souths in the atoms need to be lined up.

Key words

alloy

magnetic/non-magnetic

metal

Agree with your partner about which of these metals is magnetic.

aluminium   brass   copper   gold   iron   lead   nickel   silver   steel   tin

Make a magnet out of a steel nail

magnet

S

N

nail

1 Hold the nail flat and stroke the magnet along the nail.

2 Make sure that you only stroke in one direction.

3 Repeat this 50 to 100 times.

4 Now test the magnet you have made. How many paperclips does it pick up?

■ For more activities, go to Workbook 3 page 96.

We are going to use a magnet to test objects made of different materials.

chair leg
(steel / aluminium)

window
(glass)

table
(wood)

pan
(cast iron)

bowl
(plastic)

drink can
(aluminium)

water pipe
(copper)

food can
(steel)

Which of these things do you think is magnetic?
Can you explain your answer?

Are all metals magnetic?

Your teacher will give you a range of objects made from different metals.

1 Copy the table.

2 Use a magnet to test the objects. If the magnet is attracted, the metal is magnetic. Tick the box: Yes or No.

Object	Material	Magnetic?	
		Yes	No
chair leg	steel / aluminium		

3 Write a conclusion to your investigation.

4 Present your ideas to the class.

Warning! Do not test electronic objects such as whiteboards or computers. The magnet will damage them.

Key idea

You can use a magnet to find out which materials are magnetic.

■ For more activities, go to Workbook 3 page 97.

Electromagnets

In this lesson you will explore magnets made using electricity.

Key word

electromagnet

Why is this magnet so strong? It isn't because it is very big, so what else could make it strong?

Electricity can make very strong magnets

Recycling centres use magnets to separate aluminium and steel cans. The magnet attracts the steel cans and leaves the aluminium cans behind.

The magnet on the end of the crane is powered by electricity. This makes the magnet very strong. It is called an electromagnet.

The electromagnet in the photograph could be a million times stronger than the one you made.

When the crane driver switches off the electricity the metal loses its magnetism, so the driver can put the scrap steel down.

Where else do people use very strong electromagnets to lift things?

Make an electromagnet

We can make our own electromagnet.

1 Use the diagram to help you make an electromagnet.

2 Coil the wire around the nail 10 times. Test your electromagnet.

3 How many paperclips can you pick up?

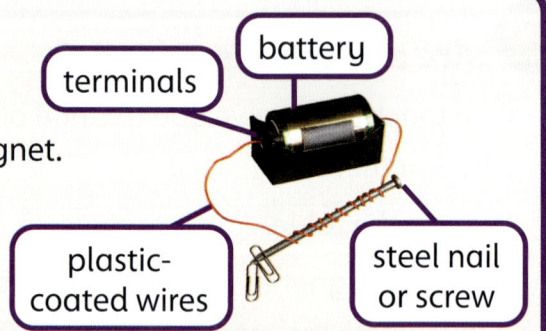

battery

terminals

plastic-coated wires

steel nail or screw

Make a stronger electromagnet

Can you make a stronger electromagnet?

1 Write a plan for your investigation. Share your plan with another group to check it.

2 Record the changes you make to your plan to improve it.

3 Carry out the investigation and record your results.

■ For more activities, go to Workbook 3 page 98.

Magnets can push as well as pull

Do you remember that the like poles of a magnet repel each other? This is how the Maglev train works. The magnets in the train and the magnets in the steel track push each other away. This lifts the train so it moves much more easily.

Magnets are used in many devices

Look at the photographs and the text boxes.
Discuss each use of magnets and match it to the correct photograph.

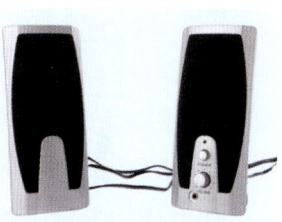

| electric drill | power station | washing machine | speakers |

1 Inside this building is an extremely big magnet that helps to make electricity.

2 Inside this device electricity makes a tiny magnet vibrate (shake). The vibrations create sound.

3 Inside this tool is an electric motor. Motors use electricity to make magnets that spin around very quickly.

4 This machine uses an electric motor to spin the washing.

In three of the photographs, electricity is used to make magnetism. Agree with your partner about which photograph is the odd one out.

Stretch zone

Design a poster to show some uses of magnets. Include the ones covered in this lesson but also find out about others.

Key idea

Magnetic force is used in hundreds of things that we use every day.

Check how much you know.
Try the questions on pages 100–101.

■ For more activities, go to Workbook 3 page 99.

4 Introducing Forces and Magnets

1 What force do you use for each of these activities?

Write a word from the word box each time.

> pull   push

   a Open a drawer: _____

   b Kick a ball: _____

   c Shut a door: _____

   d Throw a ball: _____

   e Pick up a book: _____

2 Tick the metals that are magnetic in the list below.

iron ☐   brass ☐   cobalt ☐

steel ☐   nickel ☐   wood ☐

3 Use your knowledge of magnets to predict whether these magnets will attract or repel each other. Write **attract** or **repel** under each picture.

_____   _____   _____

_____   _____

■ For more activities, go to Workbook 3 page 100.

4 Look at the diagram of the atoms in a non-magnetic metal. Draw how the atoms are arranged in a magnetic metal.

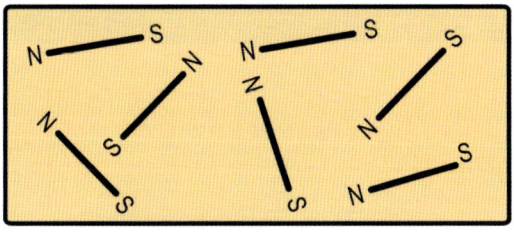

Non-magnetic metal

N [   ] S

Magnetic metal

5 **a** What happens to a toy car when you increase the pushing force? Circle your answer.

goes faster   goes slower   stays still

b How can you change the direction of the toy car?

_____

_____

c How can you make something stop?

_____

_____

d What is the name of the force between two surfaces that slows things down?

_f_ __ __ __ __ __ __ __

e What type of force is this? Underline the correct answer.

contact force   non-contact force

6 Why does a magnet make a good compass?

_____

_____

■ For more activities, go to Workbook 3 page 101.

5 Exploring Health, Skeletons and Muscles

In this unit you will:

- review the life processes of nutrition, movement, growth and reproduction
- find out that animals and humans need to get their nutrition from what they eat
- explore the signs of illness, infectious diseases and vaccinations
- find out that humans and some animals have bony skeletons
- discover that animals with skeletons have muscles attached to the bones
- understand how we use medicines.

bone   diet   exercise
food   healthy
infectious disease
medicine   movement
muscle   nutrition
reproduce   skeleton
vaccination

Look at the photograph.

With a partner, talk about what the children are doing.

Why would a healthy breakfast help them to do this?

Why do we need muscles?

Talk about which muscles you have used today.

Look at the photograph of a baby rabbit and adult rabbit.

Discuss why bones have to grow as an animal gets older.

Science fact

Scientists have shown that how long people live is closely linked to having clean water and healthy food. The amount of exercise they take is also important. Good doctors and hospitals also play a big part.

■ For more activities, go to Workbook 3 pages 102–103.

The life processes

In this lesson you will review the life processes of nutrition, movement, growth and reproduction.

Think back

List what you can remember about the life processes. Life processes are things that livings things do, which non-living things do not.

Look at the photographs.
With a partner, discuss which life processes the photographs show.

All animals and humans have to eat food and drink water to stay alive.

Eating and drinking to stay alive is called nutrition.

All animals and humans must move to find food and drink. Animals also move to get away from predators.

All animals and humans grow and reproduce to have young so that their species survives.

Science fact

Every year around 3.4 million people die from drinking unsafe water.

104

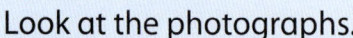

■ For more activities, go to Workbook 3 page 104.

The people in the photograph do not have enough food. With a partner, research why areas might run out of food.

Design a poster to let people know about the problems faced by people who do not have enough food.

Cleaning water

Your teacher will give you a sample of dirty water.

1 Write down what the water looks like.

2 Make a filter funnel as shown in the picture.

3 Pour the water into the filter funnel and collect the water that comes out the bottom.

4 Write down what the filtered water looks like.

5 Repeat using different materials in your filter funnel.

Which material in the filter made the water look cleanest?

Warning! Do not drink the filtered water. It may still contain harmful living things and chemicals that can make you ill.

Key idea

Humans and animals eat, drink, move, grow and reproduce.

Stretch zone

Think about where your water supply comes from. Research how it is cleaned and kept clean. Draw a spider diagram of your findings.

105

■ For more activities, go to Workbook 3 page 105.

A balanced diet

In this lesson you will explore and research the role of diet and nutrition in keeping healthy.

Some animals need to eat only one type of food. A lion might only eat meat but it gets everything it needs from the meat.

Think back

Remember your learning about herbivores, carnivores and omnivores.

Humans are omnivores. They need to eat lots of different types of food to stay healthy.

Key words
carbohydrate
diet
fat
food
healthy
mineral
protein
vitamin

vitamins and minerals – for general health, for example, to build bone and teeth

carbohydrates – give energy

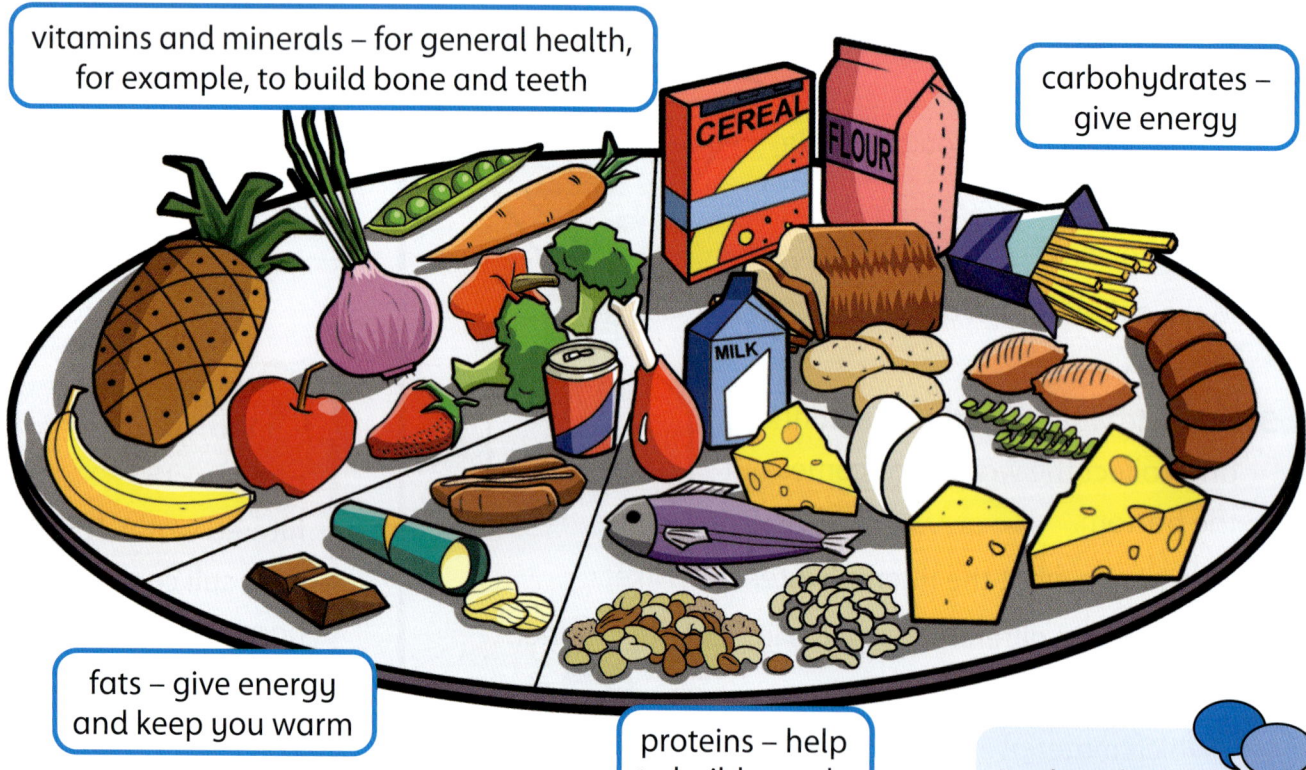

fats – give energy and keep you warm

proteins – help to build muscle

Look at the picture of the plate. With a partner, talk about the different foods you can see. List any that you have eaten over the last 24 hours.

Scientists have grouped the foods by what they do for our bodies.

The groups and what they do for our bodies is shown on the plate.

If we eat some foods from each of these groups we have a balanced diet and we keep healthy.

■ For more activities, go to Workbook 3 page 106.

Food labels

You will be given a range of food packets and tins.

1 Find the food label on each one.

2 Record how much protein, fat, carbohydrates, minerals and vitamins are found in each food.

3 Use the evidence to sort the foods into three groups:

- high protein
- high fat
- high carbohydrate.

4 Which of the following people would need to eat the most carbohydrates? Explain why:

- a marathon runner
- an office worker.

Nutrition Facts	
Serving Size 100 g	
Amount Per Serving	
Calories 250	Calories from fat 10
	% Daily Value*
Total Fat 4%	4%
Saturated Fat 1.5%	4%
Trans Fat	
Cholesterol 50mg	28%
Sodium 150mg	15%
Total Carbohydrate 10g	3%
Dietary Fiber 5g	
Sugars 3g	
Protein 16%	
Vitamin A 1% • **Vitamin C** 3%	
Calcium 2% • **Iron** 2%	
*Percent Daily Values are based on a 2,000 calorie diet. Your daily values may be higher or lower depending on your calorie needs.	

Be a scientist

Scientists use books and the internet to research information about what they are studying. These are called secondary sources of information.

▶ page 8

With a partner, discuss what you think could happen if a person did not eat enough of the right foods.
Do you know which food types you should eat in small amounts?

Science fact

Scientists measure the energy in food in units called joules or kilocalories. A 9-year-old child needs about 1800 kilocalories a day to be healthy.

Key idea

We need to eat different types of foods to help us live and grow.

Stretch zone

Design your own food label for your favourite food.

■ For more activities, go to Workbook 3 page 107.

Infectious diseases

In this lesson you will explore the signs of illness, infectious diseases and vaccinations.

Key words

illness
infection
infectious disease
microorganism
vaccination

Diseases can be caused by pathogens. These are microorganisms such as bacteria, viruses and fungi. These diseases are called infectious diseases. They can be spread from person to person. Examples of infectious diseases in humans are measles, mumps, influenza, polio and Covid-19.

What you feel when you are ill are called symptoms. What can be measured or seen is a sign. Pain is a symptom. Body temperature and your pulse rate are signs.

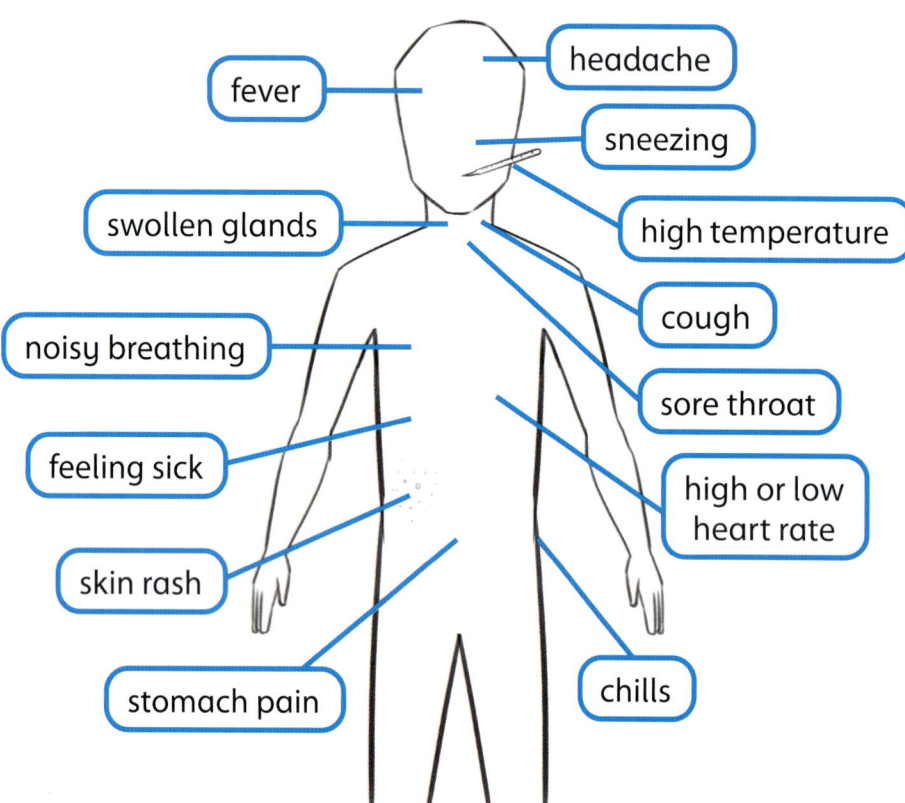

- fever
- headache
- sneezing
- swollen glands
- high temperature
- cough
- noisy breathing
- sore throat
- feeling sick
- high or low heart rate
- skin rash
- stomach pain
- chills

Talk about the diagram with your partner. Decide which labels show signs and which show symptoms. Present your ideas in a table.

With your partner, find out about an infectious plant disease found in your area. Discuss how it can be treated.

Plant diseases

Plants can also get infectious diseases. Examples are leaf spot, mildew and mosaic virus disease.

A plant with a disease may have wilted, yellow or spotty leaves and stems. It may also be covered in mould. Some plant diseases can be treated with chemicals but often the plant has to be removed and destroyed.

Staying safe from infectious diseases

1 Use the internet or books to find out how infectious diseases are spread from person to person through air, water or by touch.

2 Choose one example of an infectious disease and research how its spread can be slowed down or stopped.

3 Make a health information leaflet to advise people how to prevent the spread of the disease. Include coloured diagrams, charts and tables.

Vaccination

Animals and humans have an immune system to help fight against invading pathogens. The body makes antibodies to kill the pathogens. This can take time to start so doctors have developed a way to speed this process up. They inject weak or dead pathogens into your body to encourage you to make antibodies. This is called a vaccination. Some vaccines are given as a drop of liquid in the mouth or a spray into the mouth or nose.

If you then get infected with the pathogen after being vaccinated, your body will be more ready to attack the disease.

> Have you been vaccinated for any diseases? Tell your partner what happened.

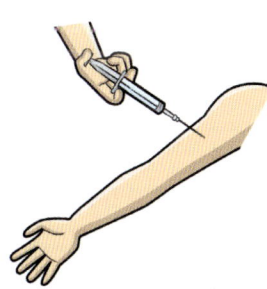
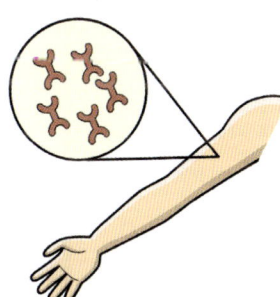

| Weak or dead pathogen is added | Body produces antibodies but not enough to make you ill | Antibodies are ready to attack the pathogen in future |

How a vaccine works

Key ideas

- Infectious diseases are caused by microorganisms. They make us ill and can cause different signs and symptoms of disease.

- Vaccinations can prevent some infectious diseases.

Science fact

Vaccines can now protect against many infectious diseases, such as chicken pox, smallpox, measles, mumps, polio, tetanus and flu. Each pathogen needs to have its own specific vaccine.

■ For more activities, go to Workbook 3 page 109.

5 Exploring Health, Skeletons and Muscles

The importance of water

In this lesson you will find out that water is an important part of a healthy diet.

Key words

cell

filter

water

Think back

What do plants need to stay healthy? Make a list.

Are these the same for animals?

All living things are made up of cells. Cells are very small structures filled with a watery liquid.

Without water the cells dry up and the life processes cannot take place.

Like plants, all animals and humans need water so their bodies can work properly. About 70% of our body is made up of water.

Humans need to drink water to replace the water we lose when we sweat, breathe out damp breath and go to the toilet. Humans can survive three weeks without food but only three to four days without water.

How much water do you drink in one day?

1 Every time you have a drink, measure out the same amount of water as the liquid you drank into a bottle or measuring jug. For example, if you have a glass of orange juice for breakfast, pour a glass of water into the jug.

2 Measure how much water you have collected at the end of the day.

Compare your amount with the amounts others in your class collected. Do you all drink about the same amount?

Stretch zone

Work out how much drinking water a family of five people would need in a week. Use the information from your investigation to work it out.

Science fact

Experts agree that about 2–3 litres of liquid a day is enough for most adults.

■ For more activities, go to Workbook 3 page 110.

It is not always easy for people to get fresh drinking water.

Some people have to walk or travel a long way to find water for their families. Some people have to drink dirty water, which can make them ill.

Testing water to find the cleanest

To compare different water samples you can use a filter funnel like the one you used on page 105.

1 Collect water from four different sources around the school.
2 Look at the water samples carefully.
3 Design a table to record your observations.
4 Pour each sample through your filter funnel. Use fresh filter paper every time.
5 Record how dirty the filter paper becomes.

Which water source was the dirtiest and which was the cleanest?

Stretch zone

Design and make a poster to explain how dirty drinking water can be made safer.

 Warning!

Never drink water that you are not sure about, even if it looks clean. Discuss why this is important.

If you had to drink water from the dirtiest source what could you do to the water to make it safer? Discuss your ideas with a partner.

Key idea

Animals and humans need water to survive.

5 Exploring Health, Skeletons and Muscles

■ For more activities, go to Workbook 3 page 111.

Planning healthy meals

In this lesson you will use your knowledge of a healthy diet to plan meals.

Key words

balanced diet
energy
fit
healthy

Think back

Make a list of the types of foods that give us energy.

This athlete needs to have a special diet to make sure she is very fit when she takes part in competitions.

What advice would you give the athlete about the meals she should eat?

To help you to decide, discuss the following questions with a partner.

- Which foods will give energy?
- Which foods will provide minerals and vitamins?
- Which foods will help to make strong bones?
- Which foods will help to keep muscles strong?

Write a short message to the athlete giving her your advice.

Science fact

An Olympic rower needs to eat 6000 kilocalories of food a day when training. That is three times more than the kilocalories recommended for a 9-year-old!

■ For more activities, go to Workbook 3 page 112.

Investigating meals

Analyse the different meals on offer in your school dining room or keep a diary of the food in your dinner.

1 List the foods that are high in:

- protein
- vitamins
- fats
- minerals.
- carbohydrates

2 Write a short report to explain whether the meals are providing you with a healthy and balanced diet or not.

Suggest some ways that they could be made even more healthy.

> Compare your ideas with the rest of the class. Are they the same or different?

Stretch zone

Plan a survey to find out what people in your class bring to school as packed lunch or as snacks.

Conclude if they are bringing healthy food.

Key idea

We can choose foods to make a healthy, balanced meal.

■ For more activities, go to Workbook 3 page 113.

Exercise and health

In this lesson you will explore and research the role of exercise in keeping healthy.

Key words
breathing rate
exercise
heart rate

Some types of exercise are running, walking, swimming and karate.
What exercise do you like doing?

Movement is one of the life processes. Many people, especially children, have active lives. This helps them to keep healthy.

As people grow older they can become less active. Some adults have jobs where they sit in the same position for a long time.

We get energy from our food. We use energy to live, work and exercise. We need to balance the energy we take in with the energy we use. This keeps us healthy.

What happens to our bodies when we exercise?

1 Before you begin, sit quietly and relax.
2 Exercise for two or three minutes. Walk quickly or jog, run on the spot, or do star jumps.
3 As soon as you stop, sit down.

How do you feel compared to when you were sitting down before the exercise? Discuss this with the group.

4 Observe the effects on another student.

Can you see what is happening to the student's chest?

 Warning!
When exercising in hot climates, drink lots of water and take care not to become overheated. At the first sign of distress, stop!

■ For more activities, go to Workbook 3 page 114.

Our heart pumps blood to every part of our body. The blood contains oxygen and sugars for energy.

When we exercise, our body needs more energy and oxygen. That is why our heart beats faster and more strongly when we exercise. Our lungs need to breathe in as much oxygen as possible. That is why we breathe more quickly during and after exercise.

How fast the heart beats is called the heart rate.

Your pulse will tell you your heart rate. Count it for 30 seconds and double the number. This gives you beats per minute

Science fact

An adult's heart beats 60 to 70 times a minute. This can rise to 150 beats a minute during exercise.

Breathing and heart rates

1 Plan an investigation to find out what happens to your heart rate and breathing rate as you exercise.

Read the warning about exercise on the previous page.

2 Carry out your investigation.

3 Record your findings in a suitable table.

Are your breathing rate and heart rate after exercise the same as everyone else in your group? Write up your conclusions.

Stretch zone

Use the internet to find out about recovery rate. Plan how you could find out your recovery rate. Compare your recovery rate to other people in your class.

Key idea

Regular exercise keeps us fit and healthy.

5 Exploring Health, Skeletons and Muscles

115

■ For more activities, go to Workbook 3 page 115.

The human skeleton

In this lesson you will understand that humans have bony skeletons inside their bodies.

Key words
bone
skeleton

The diagrams show the bones inside a person's body. All of the bones in the body together are called the skeleton.

Look at the different bones in the skeleton.
Talk about which bones are found in the arms and legs.
Now find those bones in your own arms and legs.
Say the names to each other as you find each bone.

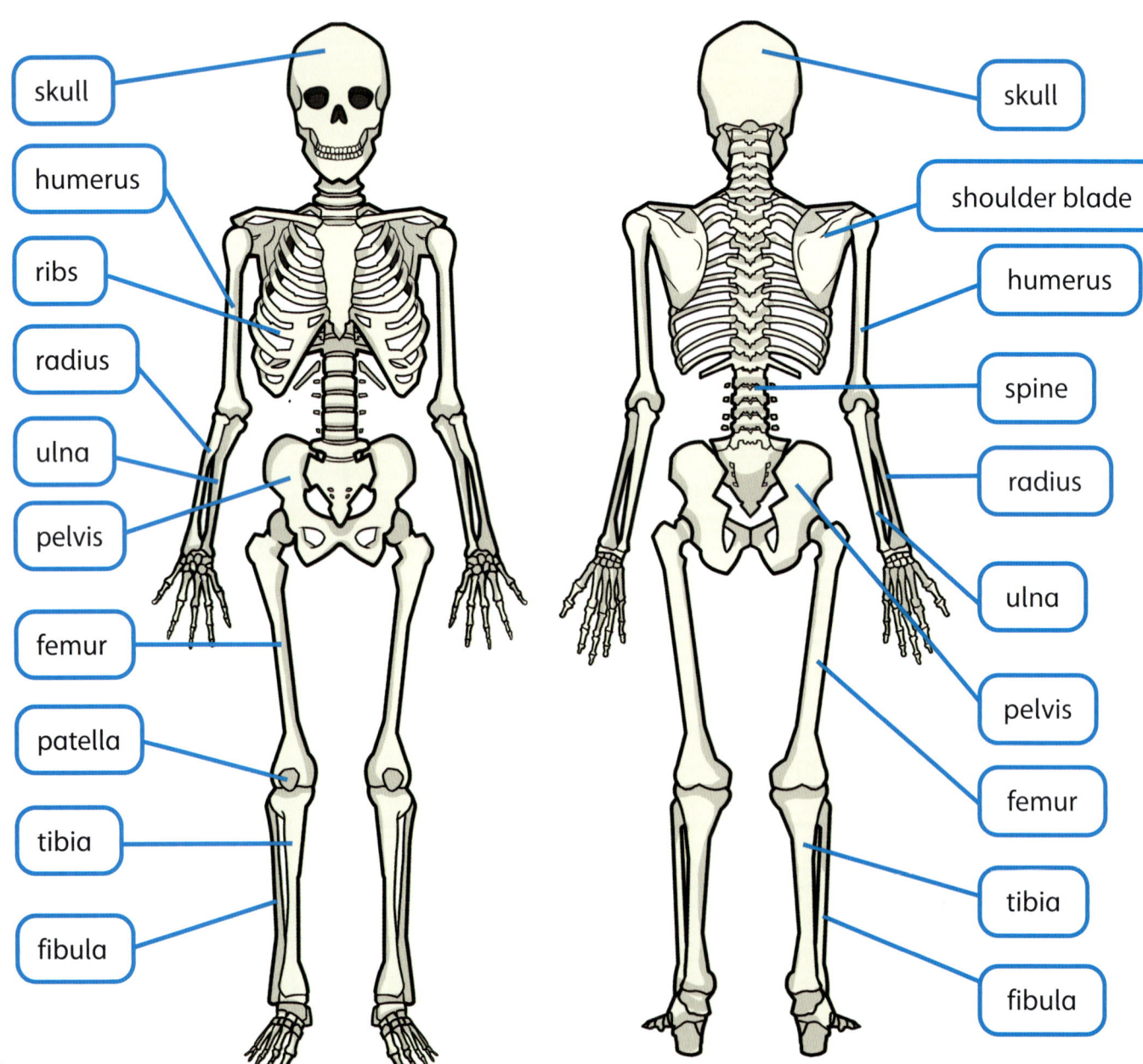

skull

humerus

ribs

radius

ulna

pelvis

femur

patella

tibia

fibula

skull

shoulder blade

humerus

spine

radius

ulna

pelvis

femur

tibia

fibula

■ For more activities, go to Workbook 3 page 116.

Skeletons are made of bones that are strong and hard.

Why do bones have to be strong and hard?

Identifying parts of your skeleton

Can you link the parts of the skeleton to the different parts of the body?

1 Work in groups. Use the diagrams of the skeleton to help you to find the parts of the body listed below.

When you have found the part of the body you must point to it and say the name out loud to your group.

skull   spine   ribs   shoulder blades   humerus   radius   ulna

femur   patella   tibia   fibula   pelvis

2 Make a body outline by drawing around a person or their shadow onto a large sheet of paper.

Work together to draw as many bones as you can into the body outline. Label each bone.

3 Display your skeleton drawing.

Science fact

Bones are not solid all of the way through. To help to make them light they have spaces inside.

Stretch zone

Think about why arms and legs do not just have one single long bone. Explain your thinking to your partner.

Key idea

Humans have many bones inside their body. These bones together are called the skeleton.

5 Exploring Health, Skeletons and Muscles

■ For more activities, go to Workbook 3 page 117.

Animal skeletons

In this lesson you will understand that some animals have bony skeletons inside their bodies.

Key words
pelvis
ribs
skull
spine
vertebrate

Think back

Point to these parts of your skeleton: skull, ribs, spine and pelvis.

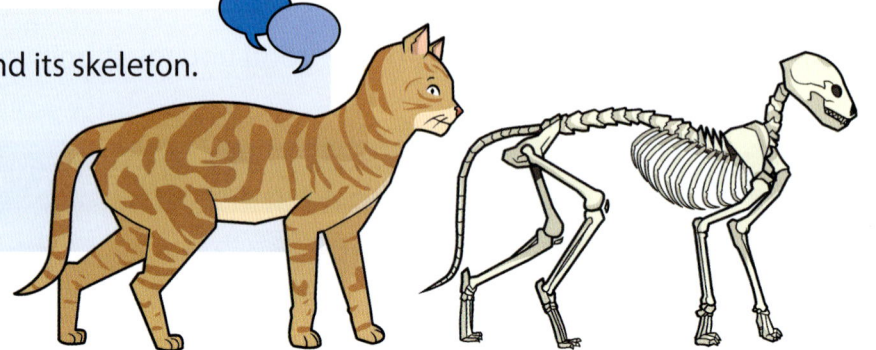

The picture shows a cat and its skeleton.
Discuss the cat's skeleton.
Point to the skull, ribs, spine and pelvis.

Some animals have a skeleton inside their body. They also have a backbone or spine. You have learned that animals with backbones are called vertebrates.

Recognising skeletons

This investigation supports the activity on page 119 of your Workbook.

1 Look at the photographs and name each animal.

2 Now look at the pictures of the skeletons. Write the matching numbers and letters in your notebook.

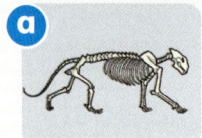 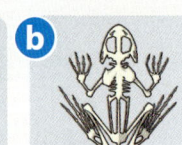 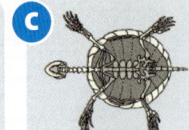   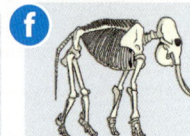

3 Discuss how the skeletons of the animals are the same.

   How are they different?

4 Find the skull, spine, ribs and pelvis in each of the animal skeletons.

■ For more activities, go to Workbook 3 page 118.

Bone is not just one material. Bones have blood vessels, nerves and living bone cells.

A hard, strong non-living material covers the outside of the bones. This makes bones into tubes.

Testing a model bone

You are going to test if bones that are empty inside are strong structures.

1 Roll a piece of paper to make a hollow tube. Stick it together with sticky tape. This is a model bone.

2 Stand your model bone up on your table. Predict what will happen to your model bone if you place an apple onto the top of it.

   Now try it.

   Was your prediction correct?

3 Add heavier objects until your model bone cannot hold them. Record the heaviest object your model bone could hold.

4 Now test your model bone to see if it is strong in another direction.

   Lay your model bone between two books and see which objects it can hold before bending.

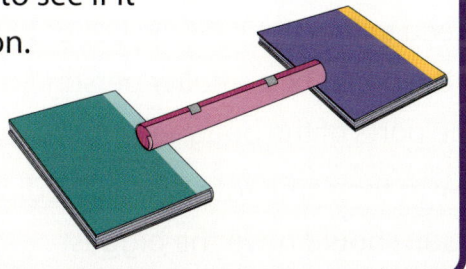

Be a scientist

Scientists share their findings to advance research. In bone science, this has led to 3D printers being used to make human-made bones to replace badly damaged ones.

▶ page 13

Bones are stronger along their length. The bones in a skeleton are linked to the way the animal moves. This is why animals have different skeletons.

Stretch zone

Write a short paragraph to explain why it is important that bones such as the leg bones are very strong along their length.

Key idea

All vertebrates have very similar skeletons.

■ For more activities, go to Workbook 3 page 119.

Skeletons need to grow

In this lesson you will learn that skeletons grow as humans grow.

Key word

grow

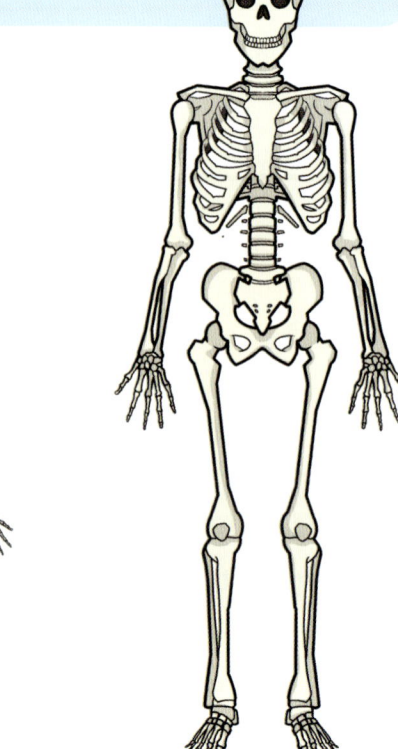
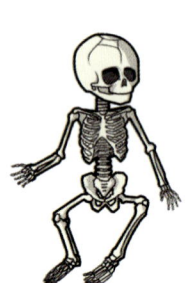
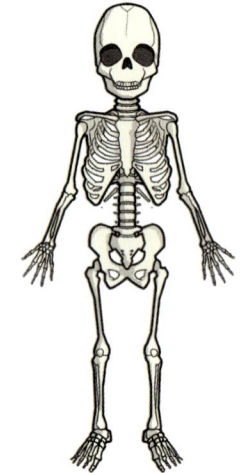

Look at the three skeletons. Which skeleton do you think is the closest to your own skeleton?

When we look at the skeletons from the baby to the adult, we notice that the skeleton of the adult is larger than the skeleton of a child. This suggests that skeletons grow. But are all the bones of a taller person bigger than the bones of a smaller person?

To answer this question, we need to find out if all the bones of a taller person are bigger than the bones of a smaller person. To do this, we need to measure some parts of the body.

If it is true that all bones grow at the same rate then a prediction would be that the tallest person should have the biggest measurements for all the different parts of the skeleton.

Do all bones grow at the same rate?

1 Plan how to measure the height, hand length, leg length and head circumference of your group.

2 Carry out your measurements.

Be a scientist

Good scientists measure at least three times and find the average (mean) of the results.

▶ page 9

■ For more activities, go to Workbook 3 page 120.

3 To record your results, copy and complete tables like these.

Height

Name of student	Height in cm
Aisha	127 cm

Hand length

Name of student	Hand length in cm
Ahmed	14 cm

Leg length

Name of student	Leg length in cm
Baserah	65 cm

Head circumference

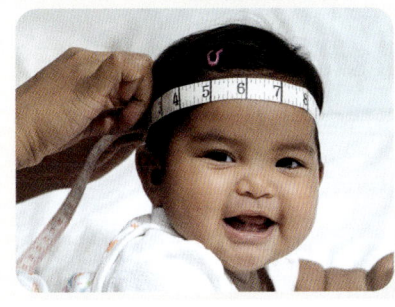

Name of student	Head circumference in cm
Hunnain	43 cm

4 Decide how you could present the results so it is easy to see patterns.

5 Work together to display your results in the most appropriate way.

6 Check your results to see if the prediction about bone growth was correct or not correct.

> What can you conclude from your investigation? Are all the bones of a taller person bigger than the bones of a smaller person?

Key ideas

- Skeletons grow as a person grows.
- Not all the bones of a skeleton grow the same amount.

■ For more activities, go to Workbook 3 page 121.

Why do we need a skeleton?

In this lesson you will learn that the skeleton supports and protects our bodies.

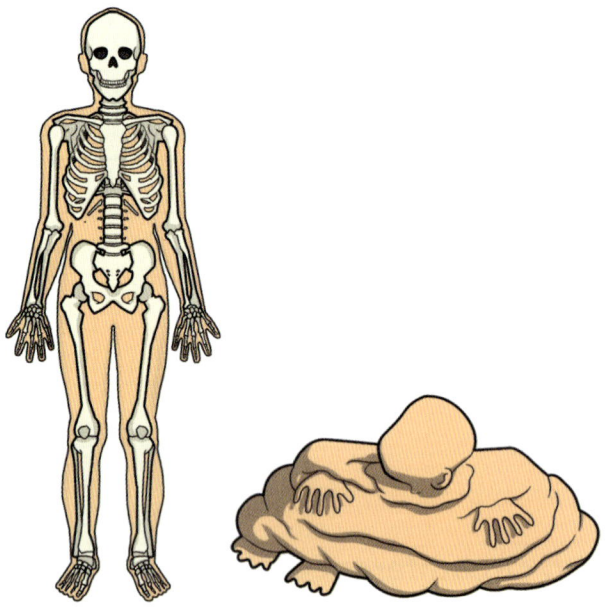

What would we look like if we didn't have a skeleton?

The functions of the skeleton are:

- to support our bodies

- to allow us to move

- to protect the organs inside our bodies, such as our heart, our lungs and our brain.

Let's look at the parts of the skeleton that protect organs.

Here are the skull and the brain. The skull is perfectly shaped to protect the brain.

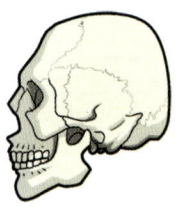 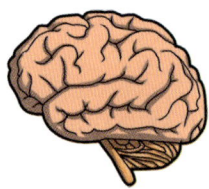 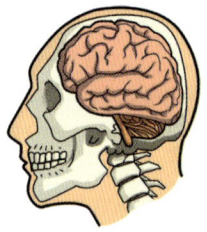

Discuss why the skull has to be strong but not too heavy.

Here are the ribs. We call this structure the ribcage.

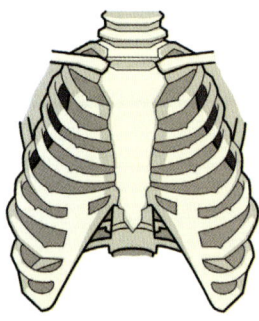

■ For more activities, go to Workbook 3 page 122.

What happens to your ribcage when you breathe in and out?

1 Place your hands on each side of your ribcage with your middle fingers touching. Take a deep breath in.

Record what happens to your hands.

Record what happens to the ribcage.

2 Breathe out.

Record what happens to your ribcage.

Discuss which organs the ribcage protects. Use the diagram below to help you.

The function of the ribcage is to protect some of the organs inside the body.

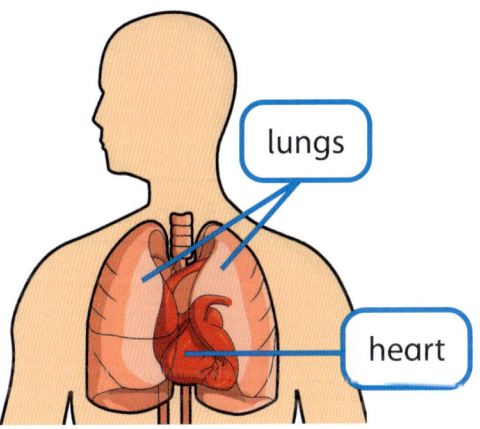

lungs

heart

This is the spine.

The spine has two main functions.

- It supports our skull and helps us to stand straight and sit straight.
- It protects the spinal cord. The function of the spinal cord is to carry messages to the brain.

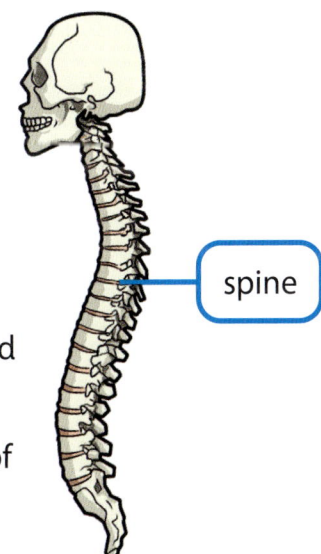

spine

spinal cord

Key idea

The skeleton supports our bodies and protects important organs such as the brain, spinal cord, heart and lungs.

Stretch zone

Research why the spine has to be split into smaller vertebrae.

What is the cushioning material between the vertebrae called? Prepare a two-minute presentation.

■ For more activities, go to Workbook 3 page 123.

5 Exploring Health, Skeletons and Muscles

Bones and no bones

In this lesson you will find out about x-rays and study some animals that do not have skeletons.

Key words

exoskeleton
fracture
invertebrate
x-ray

Think back

Study the diagram and discuss what parts of the skeleton protect the organs labelled 1, 2 and 3.

1 brain

Humans and animals with a spine are called vertebrates.

The bones of the skeleton are very hard, but sometimes they can get broken. Breaks in bones are called fractures. We use x-rays to see fractures.

2 heart and lungs

3 spinal cord

Look at these x-rays.

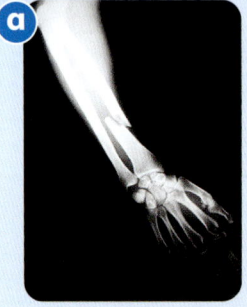

a

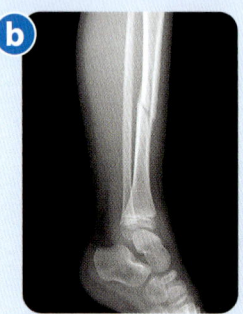

b

How do you know which bones are broken? Why are x-ray machines so important?

If we break a bone, it can be fixed. The bones are put back into place and held in place until they heal.

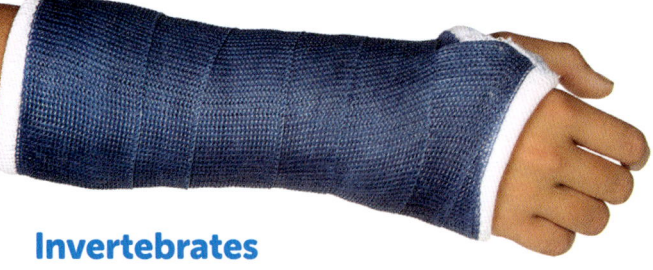

A plaster cast is helping this arm to heal

Invertebrates

Most animals do not have a skeleton inside their body. We call these animals invertebrates. Some invertebrates have no skeleton at all. Jellyfish and octopus are examples. Other animals have a hard skeleton outside their body. This is called an exoskeleton. Beetles and crabs have exoskeletons.

■ For more activities, go to Workbook 3 page 124.

1 **Jellyfish:** lives in the sea, has long tentacles

2 **Starfish:** lives in the sea, body has five parts

3 **Snail:** lives on land, has a shell on its back

4 **Spider:** makes webs, has eight legs

Discuss the descriptions of four different types of invertebrates. Match the descriptions with the photographs.

Invertebrate survey

1 Plan a survey of your local area to find and identify some invertebrates.

Decide where might be the best place to look. Carry out your survey.

2 Draw or photograph any examples.

3 Record how many of each type you observe.

Which were the most common invertebrates?

4 When you get back to the classroom, choose one of the invertebrates to research.

5 Find out its scientific name.

If it has a skeleton, find out how it uses its skeleton for support and protection.

If it doesn't have a skeleton, find out how it supports and protects its body.

6 Think of some ways that you could improve your survey to obtain more accurate results.

 Warning!
Never touch or go near to any animals you find. Why do you think this is important?

Be a scientist
Scientists use identification keys and books to help them to identify animals they do not know.

▶ page 10

Key ideas
- We can see bones using x-rays.
- Invertebrates do not have an internal skeleton or backbone.

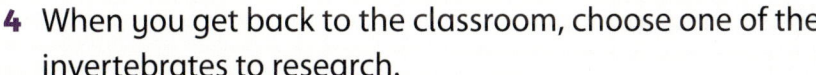

Stretch zone

Create a poster or computer presentation about your chosen invertebrate.

■ For more activities, go to Workbook 3 page 125.

Muscles and skeletons

In this lesson you will understand that animals with skeletons have muscles attached to the bones.

Key words

biceps

bone

joint

muscle

triceps

Look closely at the diagrams of the femur of a cheetah.

femur

pelvis

femur

femur

muscles

tibia

patella

muscles

What do you think muscles do?

Why do you think the cheetah needs strong muscles in its legs?

Do you think we need to have strong muscles in our legs?

Humans and animals need muscles so they can move.

We can feel muscles all over our body.

Let's try to find some muscles!

Use the diagram opposite to identify some muscles.

1 Put your left arm straight out and make a firm fist. Put your right hand on the muscle between your elbow and shoulder. Bring your fist towards your shoulder.

   Notice which muscles are moving as you do this.

2 Put your left leg straight out and move your foot up and down.

   Notice which muscles are moving as you do this.

3 Now bend your left leg at the knee.

   Notice which muscles are moving as you do this.

■ For more activities, go to Workbook 3 page 126.

We can find muscles all over our body. The diagram shows where the main muscles are. But what do they do?

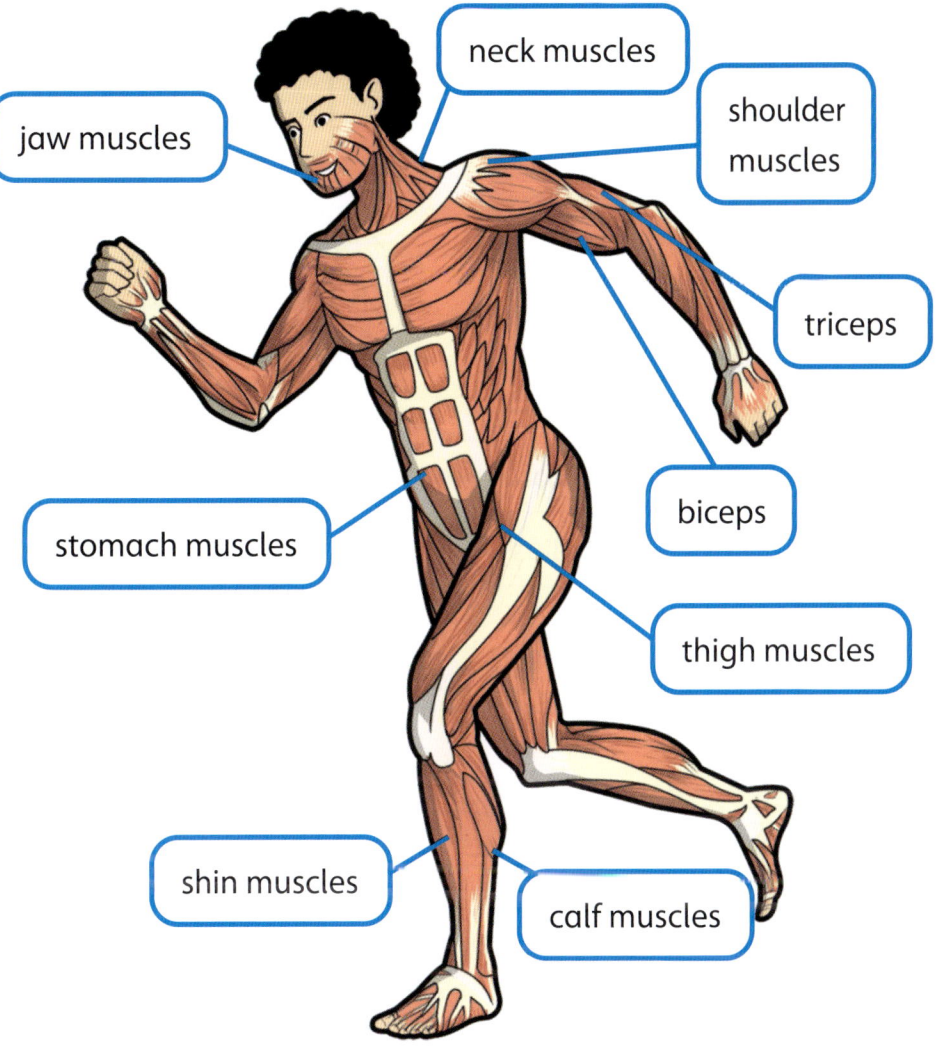

neck muscles

jaw muscles

shoulder muscles

triceps

stomach muscles

biceps

thigh muscles

shin muscles

calf muscles

Discuss which muscles are used to do each of the following activities:
● walking
● talking
● eating
● running
● breathing
● picking up a pencil
● swimming.

How do muscles work?

Bones cannot move on their own. This is why we have muscles.

Where bones meet, we have joints. For example, the elbow, the shoulder, the hip and the knee are joints. Muscles are attached to every bone. The muscles help us to move the bones. This is how we bend our arms and legs.

Science fact

There are over 650 muscles in the human body.

Key idea

Bones cannot move. They have to be pulled by the muscles that are attached to them.

Stretch zone

Research to find out examples of hinge joints and ball and socket joints in your body. Record your findings.

■ For more activities, go to Workbook 3 page 127.

How muscles work together

In this lesson you will learn that muscles contract (shorten) to make a bone move and they work together in pairs.

Key words

biceps
contract
relax
triceps

Think back

Why are muscles needed in your body?

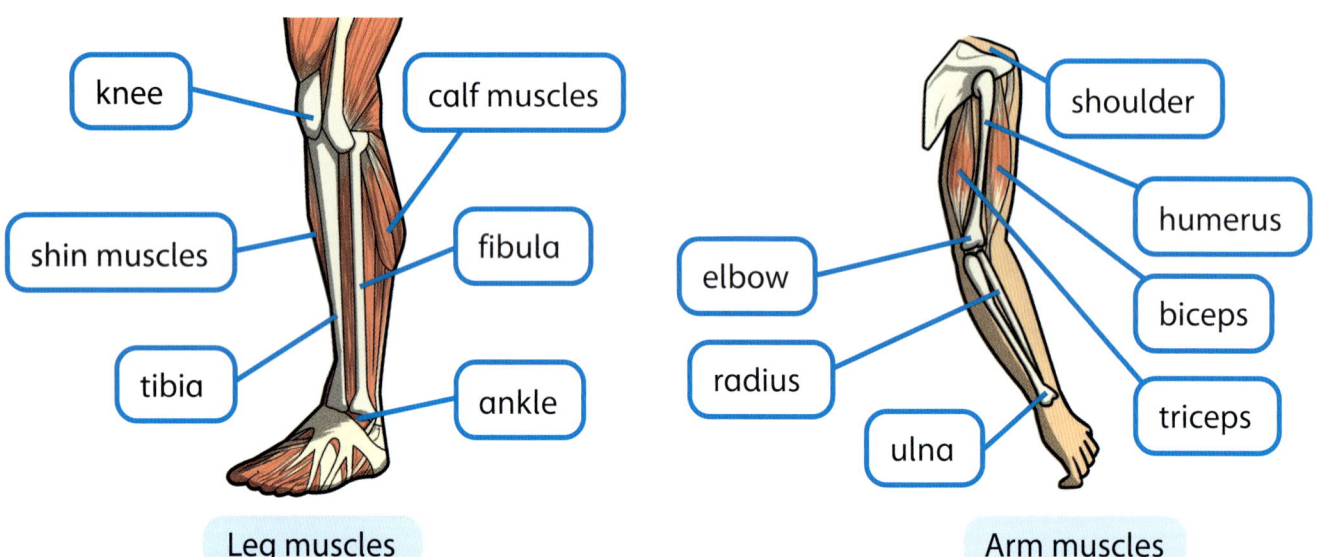

Leg muscles

Arm muscles

Discuss which muscles we use when we point our toes.

Discuss which muscles we use when we bend our arm at the elbow.

Our arm has two main muscles, the biceps and the triceps. They work together to move our arm. But how?

When our arm is straight, the biceps relaxes and the triceps contracts.

Look at the diagram. Notice the shape of the muscles.

The biceps is relaxed and is longer and thinner. The triceps is contracted and is shorter and fatter.

The function of the triceps is to pull the arm straight.

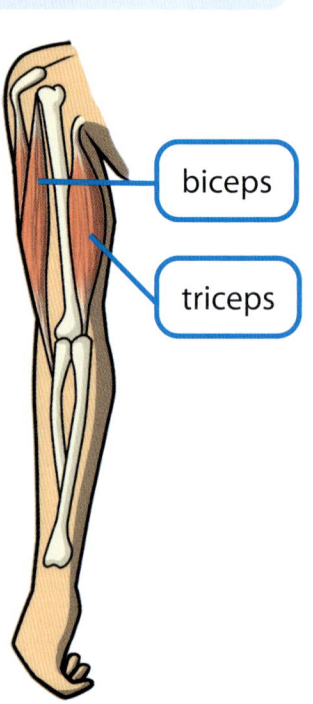

■ For more activities, go to Workbook 3 page 128.

Find your triceps

Put your left arm straight down. Use your right hand to find the triceps. You can feel it at the back of your arm.

Look at the diagram of the bent arm. What do you notice about the muscles?

When the arm is bent, the muscles look different. The biceps is shorter and fatter and the triceps is longer and thinner.

This is because the biceps is now contracted and the triceps is relaxed. The function of the biceps is to pull the bones into the bent position.

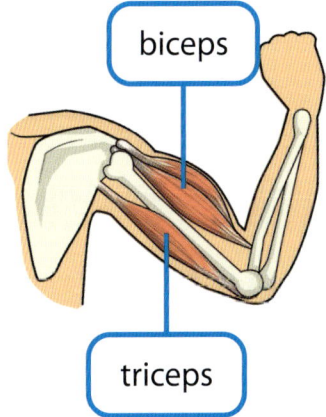

biceps

triceps

What happens to the biceps when you bend your arm?

Put your left arm straight down. Use your right hand to find your biceps muscle at the front of your left arm. Slowly bend your elbow and feel what happens to the biceps muscle. Record your observations.

Be a scientist

Scientists follow the same methods so that they can share the data and evidence they collect.

▶ page 8

Muscles work in pairs all over our body.

Science fact

Muscles cannot push. They only pull by contracting. This is why they work in pairs.

Key ideas

- Muscles contract (shorten) to pull on bones to make them move.
- Muscles often work in pairs, so one can contract as the other relaxes.

Can you think of another example where muscles work together in pairs?

■ For more activities, go to Workbook 3 page 129.

What are medicines?

In this lesson you will learn about the role of drugs as medicines.

When we feel unwell, sometimes we need to take medicines to help make us feel better.

Talk about some of the times you have felt unwell. Were you given anything to help to make you feel better?

What is a drug?

A drug is something that has an effect on our bodies. Some of these effects can be very dangerous, so many drugs cause us harm. Some drugs can help us to feel better. We call these drugs medicines.

Some medicines can cure illnesses. Some medicines can make the symptoms better.

Researching medicines

You will be asked to find out more about one of the following:

- Cough medicines

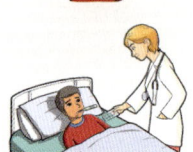

- Sore throat medicines

- Antibiotics

- Medicines for allergies

1 Use the internet and books to help you design a presentation about your chosen topic.

2 Include the names of some common medicines and how they must be used safely.

3 Download or draw pictures to make your presentation more interesting.

Science fact

The first antibiotic, penicillin, was discovered by accident. It came from some mould growing on a dish used for growing microbes. The scientist was skilled enough to see that this was useful.

Have you ever taken antibiotics? When? Why?

■ For more activities, go to Workbook 3 page 130.

Using medicines safely

It is very important to use medicines safely because if we take too much medicine, we can become unwell. Medicine labels, like the one here, have instructions about how much medicine to take and how often to take it.

Medicine label survey

Your teacher will give you some medicine labels.

1 Find the label on each box or bottle. Look carefully at each label.

2 For each medicine record in a table:

- the name
- what illnesses the medicine is used for
- how much medicine to take
- how often it should be taken
- any warnings about the medicine.

3 Design a poster to explain to other people why medicines should be used carefully.

Antihistamine

Dosage: Take 1 tablet once a day.

Warnings: Do not take if you are pregnant. May make you feel sleepy. Do not give to children under the age of 2.

Provides relief from:

☐ pet allergies

☐ hay fever

☐ skin allergies

☐ insect bites

Warning! Do not open the containers and never take medicines unless told to do so by your parents, a nurse or a doctor. Why do you think this is so important?

Key ideas

- Medicines are used to help us feel better when we are ill.
- They must be used carefully and all instructions must be followed.

Stretch zone

Research the difference between the word medicine and the word drug.

■ For more activities, go to Workbook 3 page 131.

Using medicines for a long time

In this lesson you will learn more about how medicines are used.

Key words

asthma

diabetes

medicine

Think back

Discuss three examples of medicines you have learned about. List what they are used for.

It is not always easy to know if someone has a long-term health problem because often they look very healthy.

Asthma

Asthma is a long-term health problem that affects the lungs. We use our lungs when we breathe.

Asthma can be treated with:

Inhaler

- tablets to help prevent asthma attacks
- inhalers that help someone to breathe when they have an asthma attack. Inhalers spray medicines into the person's mouth and work quickly.

When someone has an asthma attack, they find it difficult to breathe. It is very important to keep them calm and make sure they take their medicine quickly.

Look at the two children. One child has asthma. Which one do you think it is?

Researching asthma

1 Use the internet or books to find out more about asthma.

Use the questions to help you to structure your research.

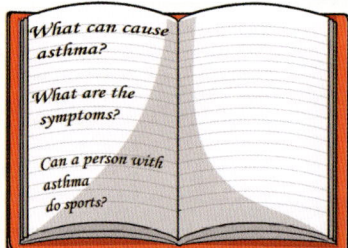

What can cause asthma?

What are the symptoms?

Can a person with asthma do sports?

2 Use your findings to design a presentation.

This could be a poster, a Wiki page or a computer presentation such as a PowerPoint presentation.

■ For more activities, go to Workbook 3 page 132.

Diabetes

People with diabetes are called diabetics. Diabetics cannot control the amount of sugar in their blood.

They need a special medicine, called insulin. They can also be careful about what they eat.

Many diabetics use a small blood test kit every day to check the sugar in their blood. A doctor shows them how to inject themselves with insulin.

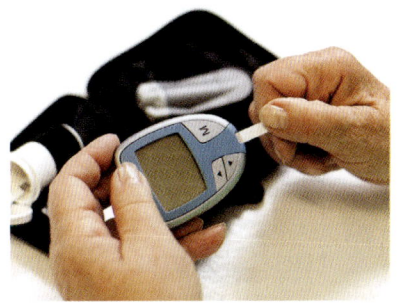

This machine tests glucose levels in blood

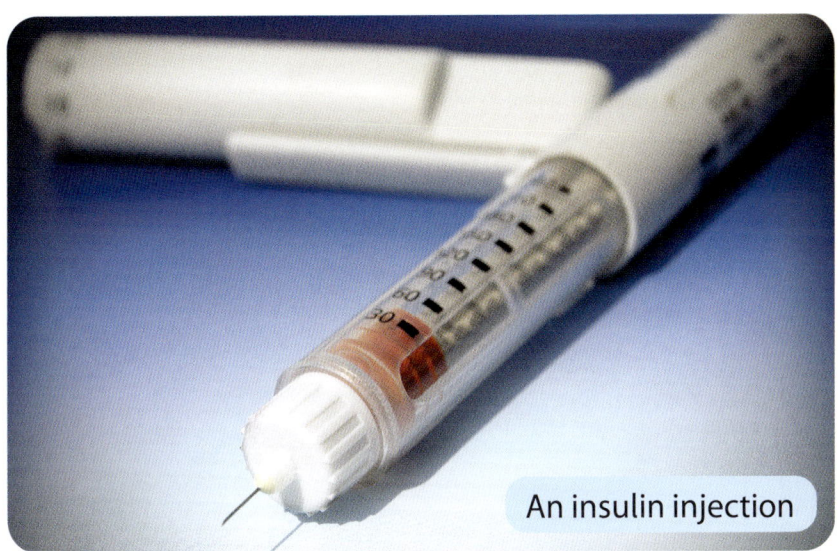

An insulin injection

Sometimes diabetes can be controlled by eating certain foods. The doctor will advise diabetics which foods to eat.

A diabetic makes regular visits to their doctor to make sure their diabetes is under control.

Stretch zone

Use the internet to find out more about diabetes. Imagine you are a doctor. Write a short letter to a person who thinks they might have diabetes. Explain what diabetes is and how it is treated. Include the words insulin, glucose, blood and foods.

Check how much you know.
Try the questions on pages 134–135.

Science fact

People were writing about the symptoms of diabetes over 3000 years ago in Egypt. They didn't have a name or a treatment for the disease though.

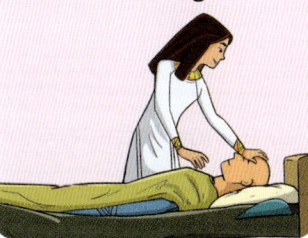

Key idea

Some illnesses, such as diabetes and asthma, need to be treated with medicines over a long period of time.

■ For more activities, go to Workbook 3 page 133.

What have I learned about health, skeletons and muscles?

1 Match each part of the skeleton with the organs that it protects. Draw a line between them.

   1 skull   **a** spinal cord

   2 ribcage   **b** brain

   3 spine   **c** heart and lungs

2 Label the bones in the leg with the correct names. Use the words in the word box.

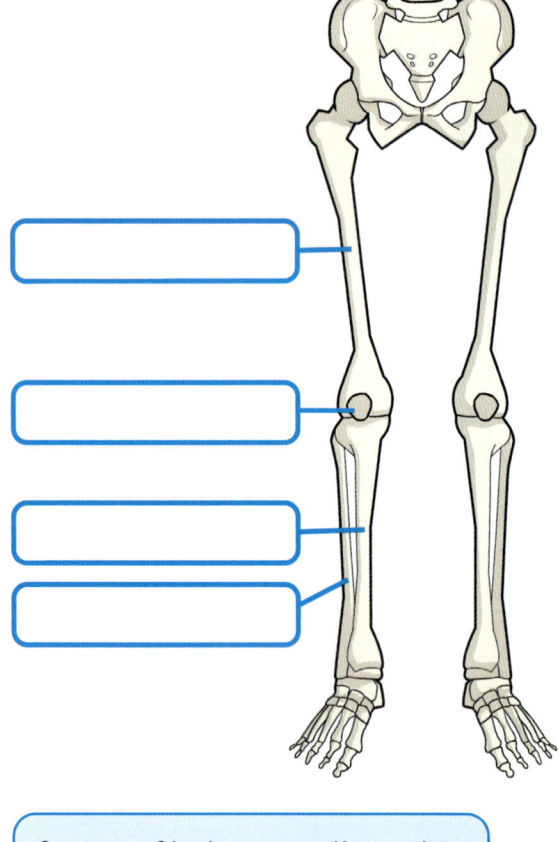

femur   fibula   patella   tibia

3 When one muscle contracts, what happens to the opposite muscle? Tick the correct answer.

it contracts   ☐

it stays the same   ☐

it relaxes   ☐

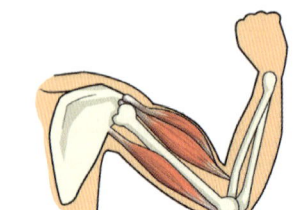

4 How can you find out how fit and healthy you are?

   You can measure your h_____ rate.

■ For more activities, go to Workbook 3 page 134.

5 **ⓐ** Fill in the missing words:

A microorganism that causes an infectious disease is called a p__ __ __ __ __ __ __.

Humans and animals can be protected from some infectious diseases by a process called v__ __ __ __ __ __ __ __ __ __.

ⓑ **Tick** the words that are **signs** a person might have an infectious disease. Now **circle** the words that are **symptoms**.

> headache   high temperature   feeling sick   noisy breathing
>
> high heart rate   stomach pain

6 Dieticians put foods into groups: healthy foods and foods that are not so healthy.

ⓐ Write down three healthy food items that you can eat lots of.

_____

_____

_____

ⓑ Write down three unhealthy food items that you should only eat in small amounts.

_____

_____

_____

7 Look at the table.

Person	Height (in centimetres)	Length of hand (in centimetres)	Length of upper leg (femur) (in centimetres)
A	117	13	29
B	130	15	33
C	128	14	32

ⓐ Which person is the tallest? _____

ⓑ Which person has the longest hand? _____

ⓒ Which person has the shortest upper leg bone (femur)? _____

ⓓ Scientists think that the height of a person is approximately 9 times the length of their hand. Do the results show this? Circle yes or no for each person.

A   yes   no

B   yes   no

C   yes   no

■ For more activities, go to Workbook 3 page 135.

Glossary

attract

bone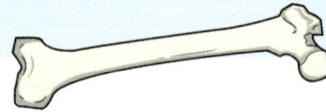

contact force

crystal

dark

diet

dispersal

exercise

flower

food

force

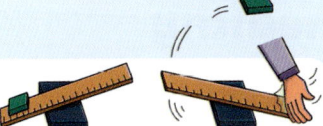

fossil

friction

grain

group

growth

healthy

infectious disease

leaf

light

magnet

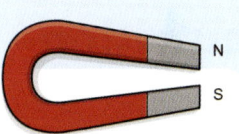
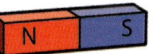

medicine

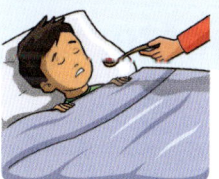

movement

muscle

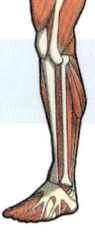

non-contact force

nutrient

nutrition

pattern

pole

pollen

pollination

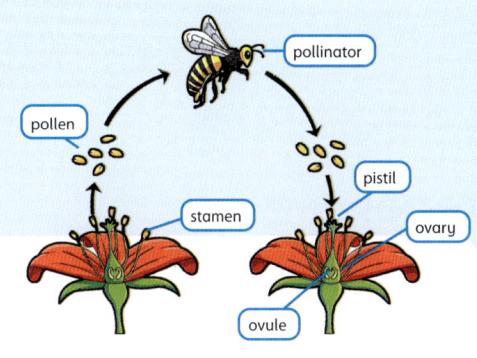

property

protect

pull

push

reflect

repel

reproduce

rock

root

sand

seed

shadow

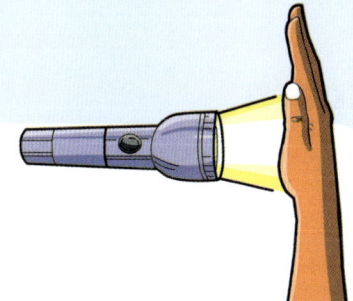

skeleton

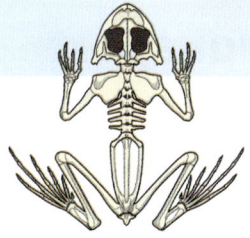

soil

stem

stone

Sun

torch

transport

trunk

vaccination

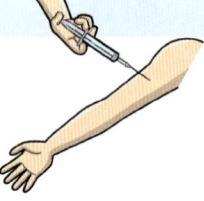

water